Techniques, Tricks, and Special F/X for Laying Down the Line

Pinstriping
Masters

Published by Nikko Press, A Subsidiary of Airbrush Action, Inc.

Executive Publisher & Editor: Cliff Stieglitz
Editor: Kate Priest
Copy Editors: Jennifer Bohanan, Michael Duck, & Laurette Koserowski
Technical Editors: Craig Fraser, Jonathan Pantaleon, Javier Soto
Production Manager: Michele DeBlock
Book Design: Jeremy Stout

Special Thanks to Bob Bond, Craig Fraser, and Ed "Big Daddy" Roth

Copyright – 2003
Second printing - 2005

First published in the United States of America by:
Nikko Press, A Subsidiary of Airbrush Action, Inc.
P.O. Box 438
Allenwood, NJ 08720
Tel: (732) 223-7878
Fax: (732) 223-2855

E-mail: ceo@airbrushaction.com
ISBN: 0-9637336-3-X
Printed in Singapore

Table of
Contents
(artists)

Introduction

The art of the pinstripe is one of the oldest techniques in the kustom painting industry. Practiced by many but mastered by few, pinstriping is an art form that combines precision skill with design simplicity, whether you're looking at a brilliant panel jam from Bob Bond or a two-color masterpiece from Von Franco.

The purest art form in the kustomizing industry, pinstriping straddles the fence between practical application and art. It is often the last thing a painter adds to a vehicle, but far from being just an afterthought, quality pinstriping can elevate a vehicle to show-winning status.

Pinstriping is the old-world art form of the hot rod industry and the true heart of the kustom kulture. Although airbrushing has become very mainstream, pinstriping has remained largely an underground art form. Many of the tricks and techniques of the trade are relatively unknown to those outside the industry. As part of a thriving subculture, pinstripers even have their own organization, the Pinheads. Stripers are an integral part of all kustom painting, but they stand apart from most kustomizers and painters. While all stripers can paint, few painters can stripe. Yet even with all the panel jams, Pinhead events, kustom kulture art shows, and Ed Roth's yearly Rat Fink Reunions, there are few books out there documenting these artists and their work.

Not surprisingly, the main players in the pinstriping industry are a unique breed. These stripers are accomplished practitioners in an industry that demands best-quality work at top speed. Their jobs call for stunningly intricate—yet surprisingly minimalist—line work. While many regard Roth and Kenneth "Von Dutch" Howard as the pioneers of pinstriping, they were actually the pioneers of the "kustom" striping era. Pinstriping was around centuries before legendary kustom artist "The Baron" had even striped his first Studebaker. Rooted in early heraldry and crest design, pinstriping dates back to a time when cars didn't even exist. The first striping jobs decorated royal carriages and chariots. The artists of striping, whether they're part of the new crowd or the old school, are tied together by a common thread: the brush and the art of the line.

We dedicate this book to the art and artists of the pinstriping world. In showing the individual pinstripers' tricks and techniques, we are also showing their contribution to the industry and the personal interpretation of the art form itself. Many of the contributing artists in this book have also given a little history about themselves and their experience in the industry. This collection of step-by-step articles is the first of its kind, showing the signature tricks and techniques of the top pinstripers in the industry today. More than just a technical manual, this book is a historical documentation of the artist and his art. It is a living tribute to the quintessential kustom kulture art form and the individual legends who have made it so.

Paint to live, live to paint

—Craig Fraser

Choosing and Using Your Brush

By Jimmy C

Pinstriping brushes come in many sizes—the bigger the number, the thicker the brush and wider the line. If you're new to pinstriping, start with a #1 or #2 brush. The bigger brush holds more paint, and many beginners have a tendency not to put enough paint on the brush. In reality, you must concentrate on putting paint on your surface, not on your brush. The paint on your brush, however, is very important. It can't be too thin or too thick. It should have just a little drag for the brush to work properly. That means you have to "palette" constantly. Paletting is the single most important aspect of pinstriping. (Basically, paletting means working the brush back and forth on a surface, while alternately dipping it in the paint. This loads the paint into the brush, allowing the brush to pull long even lines.) Not everyone holds the brush the same way—go with whatever feels comfortable for you. But everyone has to "load up" the brush on the palette. You can't paint if your brush doesn't have any paint on it! Practice and palette!

Pinstriping Guru of the Legendary Beam Brothers
Ron Beam

SUPPLIES

PAINT MEDIA: 1-Shot® Lettering Enamel
BRUSHES: Mack striping brushes, French Master lettering quill
OTHER: PPG DX-330 degreaser, 3M™ masking tape

Based in Bakersfield, California, Ron Beam and his brothers have made their mark in kustom painting and pinstriping for the past 25 years. "The Beam Brothers" are known for their incredible work on boats, race-cars, and bikes, creating some of the hottest paint jobs to come out of California in the 1970s and '80s. Their masterpieces graced the show circuit back in the days of the R.G. Canning and World of Wheels shows. If you grew up in central or southern California, you had to have a Beam Brothers paint job on your race-car or street machine. While the Beam Brothers team no longer exists, the individual brothers are still doing their own thing. In fact, the business has spread within the family. Bob, the airbrusher, has a sign business in Las Vegas, while his son, Jason (Ron's nephew), has resurrected the Beam racing logo under his fast-growing helmet painting company. With many off-road and racing professionals as clients, Jason Beam is successfully following in the family's footsteps.

Today Ron is one of the hardest working pinstripers in central California. During the last decade, he has been balancing his time between kustom work and dealership pinstriping, and he's even in demand on the racing circuit. Since Ron is equally good at one-off kustomizing and lightning-fast production stripe work, he remains one of the most sought after stripers in the region. At one point, he had so much work from his regular clientele that he put a message on his answering machine stating that he was out of business! Fortunately, that didn't work. People just showed up at the shop peeking in to see if he could cram in one more striping job.

When it comes to rock-solid straight lines, no one touches Ron. Follow along as he demonstrates some of his trademark pinstriping, including his famous "Fresno Stripe."

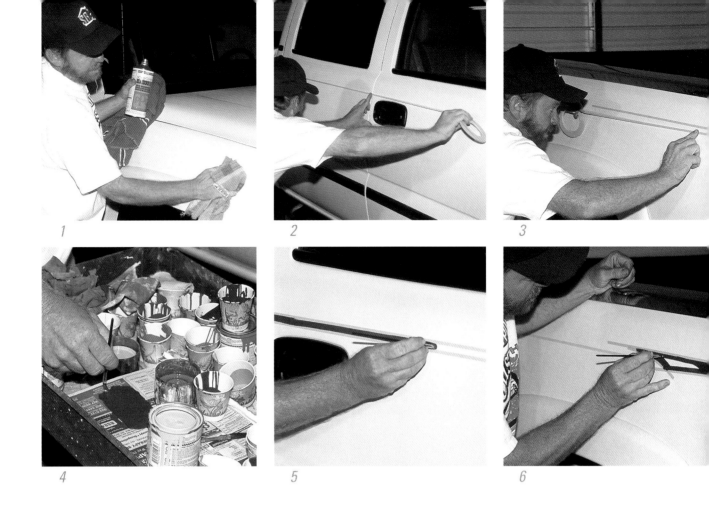

1

2

3

4

5

6

Step 1

Before any striping job, Ron wipes the entire surface down with a good degreaser. In this case, PPG DX-330 does the job. This product removes road grime and takes off any wax on the surface that may prevent the paint from sticking. After using DX-330, you should remind the owner of the vehicle to wax the surrounding area again after the job is finished and dry.

Step 2

Using 1/4-inch 3M green tape, Ron lays out the basic graphic "thick" line. This tape works well to guide the paint, and it's also very easy to pull off the tape and reposition it when making long straight lines. While the blue fine line tape may turn corners better, the green stuff leaves behind less adhesive residue.

Step 3

Ron gives himself room for a stripe that is about 3/8-inch wide and masks it off for painting. For this part, Ron opts to eyeball the line instead of measuring it out. When you've been striping as long as Ron has, your eye is as good as any ruler.

Step 4

Mixing up a batch of 1-Shot Fire Red, Ron palettes his brush and paint on the nearest phone book. Keeping the paint in a cup saves the can from drying out. Ron will often dip some catalyst and reducer on the brush to help the paint dry faster and flow better.

Step 5

Using a #3 French Master lettering quill, Ron brushes in the main graphic stripe.

Step 6

The main graphic flares into a wedge-shaped design on the back of the bed. Ron uses the brush to freehand the inside area.

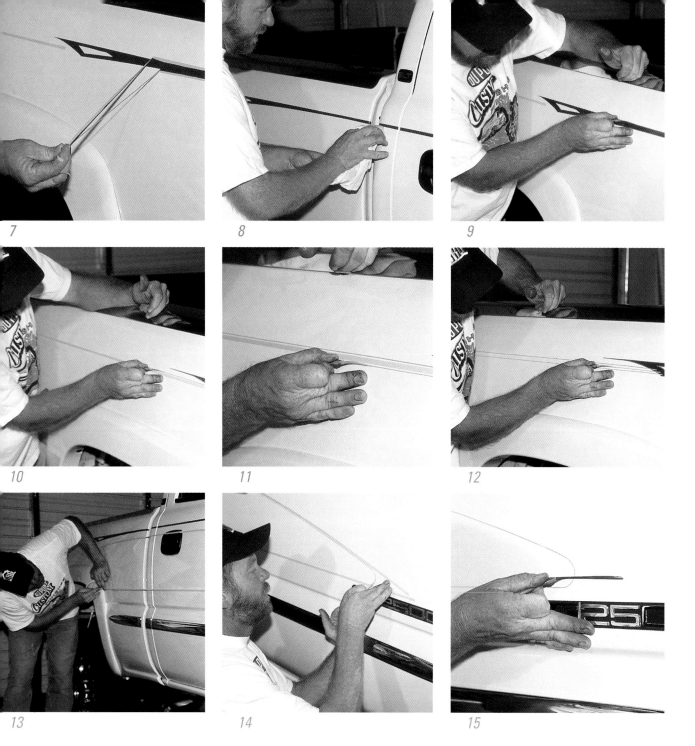

7

8

9

10

11

12

13

14

15

Step 7

Ron pulls the tape before the paint completely dries. Although you have to be careful when doing this, it's well worth it—the edge will soften on its own if the paint is still pliable.

Step 8

With all the striping unmasked, Ron cleans up any mistakes with a rag and some precleaner. It's best to catch these mistakes early on, before the paint has a chance to dry.

Step 9

Mixing up a dark gray, Ron begins pulling the border lines with his #00 Mack sword striper. Here's the famous Fresno Stripe—border stripes over a thicker center line.

Step 10

After laying another piece of tape behind the graphic, Ron adds a bit of white to the gray to get a lighter shade and begins pulling some parallel lines. He runs his finger along the tape edge to guide him as he stripes.

Step 11

Using the tape as a visual guide, Ron pulls a similar line along the bottom edge of the tape.

Step 12

After pulling the tape, Ron pulls a third line between the two. Multiple parallel lines help fill space and emphasize the linear design.

Step 13

Ron decides to add one of his single-line graphics in the space between his Fresno line and the body trim of the truck. Using the same 1/4-inch tape, he lays out the guidelines.

Step 14

Using the same #00 sword striper, Ron palettes the brush with an even lighter version of gray and traces the outline of his guide tape design.

Step 15

Going back to red, Ron lays in some cool tear-drop scallops along the leading edge of the gray single-line graphic.

Step 16

Ron uses the gray to outline and emphasize the teardrop graphic.

Step 17

Ron uses the same red and gray to spice up the top graphic with a little "hoop-d-do."

Step 18

Here's the finished classic Fresno striping job. The simple Fresno line may not be as radical as some of Ron's hot rod paintwork, but it definitely pays the bills, especially when you can crank lines out as fast as Ron can!

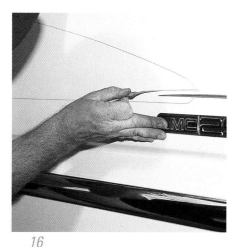

16

17

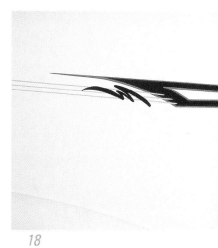

18

Ron Beam

11

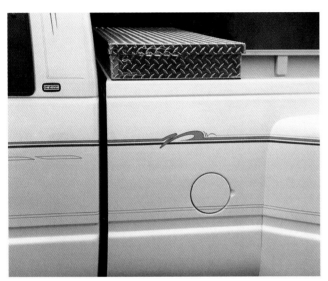

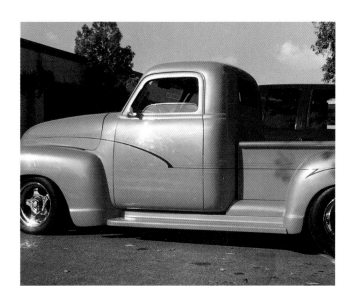

Gold Leafing on Fire Engines
Bob Bond

Bob Bond has been pinstriping, lettering, and airbrushing for more than three decades. He has decorated many motion picture vehicles for George Barris, "The King of the Kustomizers," in addition to applying the finishing touches on vehicles for celebrities including Bob Hope, Annette Funicello, Cher, Barbra Streisand, Andy Griffith and many others. His work has appeared in most major automotive and trade magazines. He has also been commissioned by many U.S. cities to restore the gold leaf ornamental striping on their historical fire engines. Bob has lectured on the art of pinstriping throughout the U.S., Canada, Mexico, and at the famous Petersen Automobile Museum in Los Angeles. He is currently the editor and publisher of AutoArt magazine, which is distributed worldwide.

When you hear the word "pinstriping," you probably think of thin lines or designs on cars. But historically, pinstriping predates the 19th century invention of the automobile. In fact, some of the very first horse-drawn fire engines ever built featured some sort of decoration. Therefore, no book on pinstriping would be complete without a section devoted to gold leaf striping on historical fire equipment. As anyone in the field can attest, gold leafing a fire engine is the ultimate task.

Pricing Guidelines

Some stripers have called me over the years to tell me that they have an old fire engine job to do, and they have no idea how to price it or even how to determine how long the job will take. My advice is to price the job by your desired hourly rate, plus material costs. This helps cover extra lines or designs that your client may wish to add as the job progresses, as well as extra time for a second coat of clear. The exact amount of time it will take depends on how proficient you are at freehand striping and applying gold leaf.

I can examine a photo and come pretty close to guessing how many days it will take and how much gold it will consume. But keep in mind, I've now gold leafed over 50 fire engines. If I have to quote a price up front, I'll give a range of about $2,500 to $3,000. Keep track of your hours, because halfway through the job you can do the math to see if you've underestimated or overestimated the hours needed. If you're way over the estimated halfway mark, you can approach the person in charge of the project and explain that the price is probably going to be higher than expected. If this is your first fire engine, estimating hours is going to be a difficult thing. Naturally, if the job only entails gold leaf stripes and no ornamental work, it can be completed in far less time than a job containing intricate scroll patterns. When estimating a job like this up front, cover your tail by adding a few extra days. Some fire engines I've worked on have taken a number of years to finish because I worked on the parts as they were completed during the restoration process. At other times, the fire engine was complete except for the decoration, but this can be a bummer because, in such instances, some parts have to be removed or taken apart before the job can begin.

Reference and Layout

Before you begin striping, you must first research the restoration. For this type of job, gathering reference material is essential to achieving accuracy. A good source for reference photos is *Enjine-Enjine* magazine, published by the Society for the Preservation and Appreciation of Antique Motor Fire Apparatus in America (SPAAMFAA). You can also check out their website *www.spaamfaa.com*. Other sources include old newspaper articles or your local fire department. Books I recommend are *American Fire Engines Since 1900* by Walter McCall, and *A Pictorial History of the Fire Engine, Volumes 1 and 2,* by Matthew Lee.

Applying the Glue for Gold Leaf

There are several companies that make glue for gold leafing. I've found that 1-Shot's new Quick Size #4008 works the best. It sets up in about one hour and can stay at the right tack for a few more hours. I always strain the Size into a cup, and then I add a small amount of Crescent superfine bronzing powder and a minute portion of Smoothie (the Smoothie is a fish-eye remover and the bronzing powder helps make the transparent sizing glue visible when you

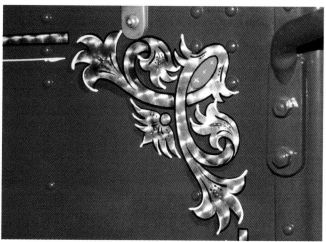

paint). I apply the Size with a good-quality #10 lettering quill from Mack. Remember, when applying Size, always start from the bottom of the design and work your way up. This way, when you apply the gold leaf, flakes of gold won't drop into the wet glue below. At this point, you should note the time when you applied the Size to an area. Wait about 30 minutes; then remove the pieces of tape very carefully to avoid smears or smudges.

Applying the Gold Leaf

This is the most critical part of the job. After approximately one hour, you should test the sized area to see if it's dry enough to apply the gold. I do this by lightly touching the glued area with my knuckle, which prevents me from leaving any fingerprints. The glue should be set up but not dry. Try to catch the glue just before it dries when it has a very slight tack. It should be sticky to the touch, but it should not come off on your finger.

I like to use 23-carat patent gold, which comes adhered to thin sheets of tissue, making it easy to apply. For best results, I hold the sheet in place with one hand and rub the gold onto the glue with a finger from my other hand, being careful not to skip or smear the gold. A trick I use when rubbing gold into place is to touch my nose to get just a little bit of oil

onto my finger; this helps my finger slide across the tissue sheet. After applying the gold to all glued areas, lightly rub the edges, breaking off little pieces of gold. This is why you should apply the Size and the gold to the bottom sections first!

Engine-turning

In some cases, fire departments prefer an "engine-turned" effect in the gold leaf. Also known as a spun aluminum effect, this is a technique for etching a pattern of overlapping circles into the gold. Immediately after adhering the gold to the glue, place a cotton ball in a piece of velvet and tape it shut at one end. Then simply push the flat portion of the velvet onto the gold and rotate your hand clockwise about half a turn. Make sure to overlap the spins so one circle starts in the center of the last one. Most people say the spins in the gold make all the difference in the world and really make the design pop out.

Hints on Applying the Pinstripes

When I paint long straight lines, I first tape off a guideline next to the gold leaf line using 1/4-inch masking tape. While painting, I'm resting my outer fingers on the tape's edge, keeping the line close and parallel to the guide tape. If a single piece of masking tape isn't thick enough to guide your finger, simply double- or triple-up on the tape layers for more grip. This works very well on long straight horizontal lines.

Extra Details

The scroll designs found on fire engines date back to Roman times, when they were used on pillars and carvings. Even old-style dollar bills contain intricate vine-like scroll patterns, which are based on the acanthus plant. I like to give my designs a look that's both three-dimensional and historically accurate by using shadows, interlacing effects, highlights, and small details. Some scroll designs on historic fire engines contain a fade-away transparent tinted color, which creates the shadows. This is achieved by paletting clear onto the brush, then dipping one side of the brush into asphaltum shading and repaletting to achieve a clear-to-color fade brush-stroke on the palette. Note: Palette onto a piece of brass or gold vinyl to see the fade as it will appear on the gold before you apply it "for real."

Tips on Clearcoating

The clear over the gold leaf is not permanent. I recommend to all owners of fire engines that I've gold—leafed to reclear the gold areas every few years. I also tell them to keep an eye on the clearcoat—if it starts to feel rough and no longer slick, this is the first sign that the clear is starting to go bad. In this case, the design should be clearcoated right away. Doing this periodically will ensure a long life for the gold leaf. Fire engines on display in museums may never have to be cleared again. Rigs that are used daily have to be checked regularly and maintained.

Bob Bond

Pinstriping a Pick-Up Truck
Julian "Mr. J" Braet

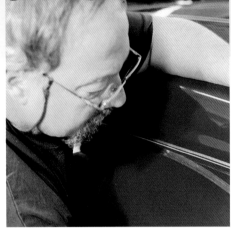

SUPPLIES

PAINT MEDIA: 1-Shot® Lettering Enamel
BRUSHES: #0 Xcaliber striping brushes
OTHER: Rapid-Prep wax and grease
    remover, masking tape, Stabilo
    pencil, magnetic guide, Xcaliber Art-
    Kups, 3M™ Fine Line masking tape
    (#215), aluminum ruler

Julian "Mr. J" Braet has been a well-known figure in the automotive graphics and sign industry for more than 25 years. His unique airbrush lettering and pinstriping has been instrumental in spreading the "Jersey Style" all over the United States and beyond. Though Braet hails from the East Coast, most of his "kustom kulture" influences were from California. "I had some great teachers," he said. "I would buy the latest car books for a quarter, and had at my fingertips work done by the masters in California. Influenced by the late Ed "Big Daddy" Roth, Von Dutch, Stanley Mouse, Dean Jeffries, Larry Watson, Tommy the Greek, and of course, the East Coast's own Andy Southard, I would practice striping on anything that would stay still—much to my parents' dismay—which included some furniture." After graduating from high school, Mr. J met up with sign painter Tony Anthony, who let the young artist apprentice in his shop.

Although Mr. J owns his own lettering and graphics shop in New Jersey, he still finds time to write articles for the top trade magazines, such as *Sign Business, SignCraft, Signs of the Times,* and *Airbrush Action.* In addition to his writing, Mr. J teaches pinstriping and airbrushing workshops at international and national trade shows, and Letterhead and Pinhead events. Mr. J's extensive experience in pinstriping and lettering has enabled him to develop unique tools for artists, custom painters, and anyone else interested in becoming the best in their craft.

For this project, Mr. J will stripe the sides, hood, and tailgate of a 2001 Ford "crew cab" pick-up truck in three colors.

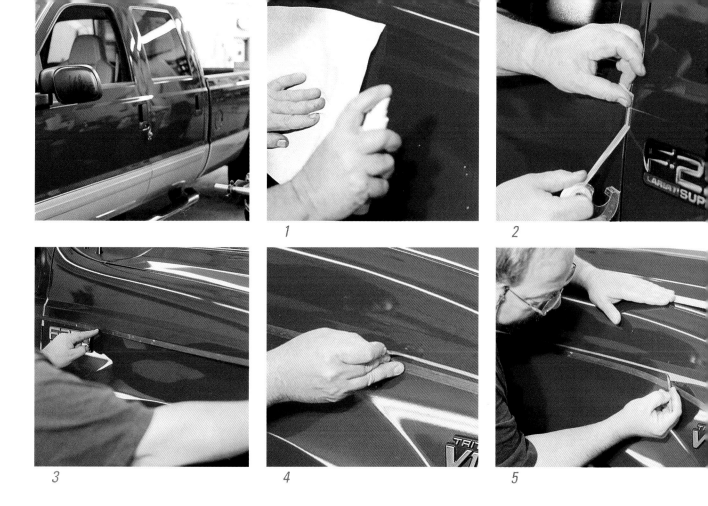

1

2

3

4

5

Step 1

Before doing any layout or painting, I use Rapid-Prep wax and grease remover. This is a water-based product that is safe to use and very effective in preparing any surface for paint. Note: Prepping the surface is one of the most important steps. If you don't take the time to thoroughly clean the surface, the paint may not adhere properly.

Step 2

I apply a small piece of Scotch® tape between the door gaps to create a clean edge. If you look closely, you can see the white line that I've drawn with a Stabilo pencil just above the emblem. This is a guideline for the magnetic tape.

Step 3

I use a magnetic guide as a straightedge to pin-stripe the sides or any other long stripes on the truck. It's 1/2-inch wide, flexible, and works perfectly on any "steel" surface.

Step 4

Now stripe the first color with 1-Shot metallic gold. I add a couple of drops of 1-Shot Hardener (#4007) to 1-Shot High Temp Reducer (#6002). I use a #0 Xcaliber striping brush to lay down the first line. Notice the placement of my fingers in relation to the magnetic guide. I also use Xcaliber's Art-Kups— 1-ounce clear plastic, graduated cups that don't contain any wax. They're also solvent proof, so they can be used with any paint or reducer.

Step 5

I fill in the tip with the striping brush. You can also use a lettering brush or scrolling quill to do this.

Julian "Mr. J" Braet

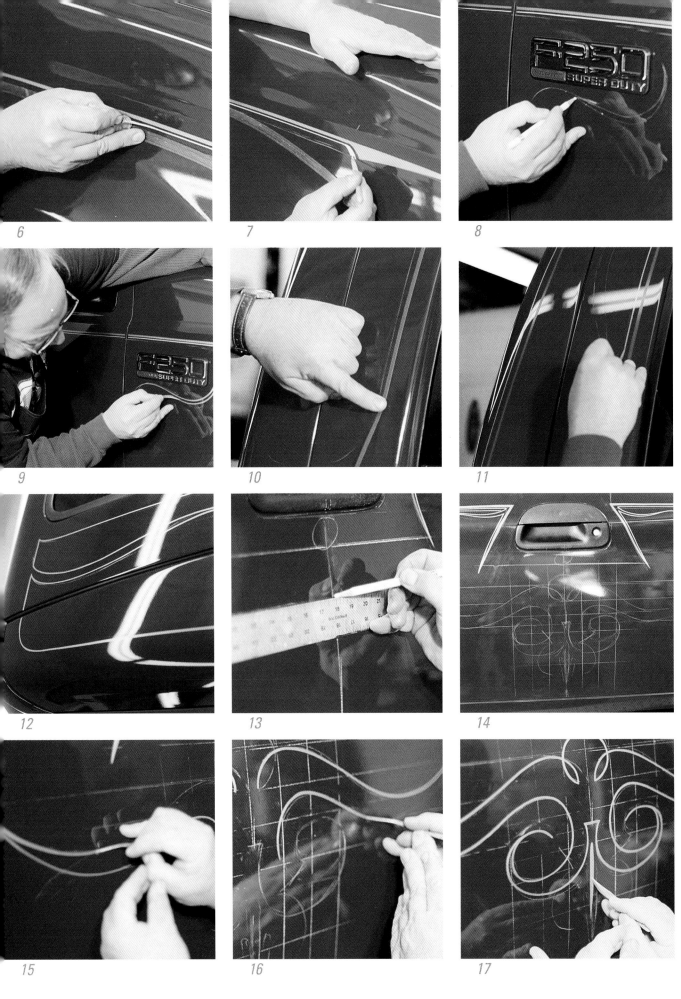

6

7

8

9

10

11

12

13

14

15

16

17

Step 6

Using the same #0 Xcaliber striping brush, I apply the second color, 1-Shot Metallic Silver, to which I add some 1-Shot Lettering White. The white gives the silver more body and helps increase its ability to cover. When applying this color, I use less pressure on the brush.

Step 7

Now I add the silver accent to the tip.

Step 8

I lay out some scrolls under the emblem. I usually stripe the sides and any straight lines first. Next I'll lay out the fancy stuff with a Stabilo pencil. This pencil is very similar to a crayon, only the Stabilo is water-based and won't harm the surface or the striping paint. Be careful when using these pencils on freshly painted areas; they could stain the surface. Always test them first on an inconspicious area.

Step 9

I switch to a #00 Xcaliber striping brush for the scrollwork. Notice how clean the lines are at the door gaps where I used the tape.

Step 10

Moving on to the sail panel, I lay out the design with the Stabilo pencil and follow up with 3M Fine Line tape as a guide for my fingers. (You can also use 1/4-inch masking tape as a guide instead.)

Step 11

Using the tape as a guide for my fingers, I apply the gold stripe.

Step 12

I stripe all of the gold first, which allows the paint to set up. I will add the accent colors later.

Step 13

I use an aluminum ruler to lay out the tailgate. The ruler has two strips of 1/2-inch magnetic material glued to the back, which comes in very handy. On any pinstriping job, I always accent one part of the vehicle a little more than the rest of it. On this job, the client wanted a large design on the tailgate.

Step 14

This is the design that I came up with for the tailgate. It's sort of a mix of Von Dutch and Mr. J! You can see the grid that I use to help me paint the design.

Step 15

I stripe the design, working from the left side. With the Stabilo lines as a guide, I follow the design as closely as possible. Note the position of my hands.

Step 16

Now I move over to the right side of the design. I constantly check left to right to make sure I'm not changing the layout. Try to keep the design as uniform as possible without making it look like a decal. Don't forget that this one is done by hand, and that's the real appeal!

Step 17

I like to add a couple of Tommy the Greek-style teardrops. Tommy is probably one of the greatest pinstripers of our time. I had the pleasure of meeting him a few years ago at his shop in Oakland, California. At that time, he was a very young 80 years old! His teardrops not only look great in this design, but they also let me pay homage to a hero of mine.

Step 18

I add a couple of lines to the bottom to bring the design together. You can see how I use the full brush here, not just the tip.

18 a

18 b

19 a

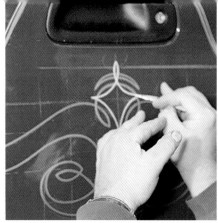

19 b

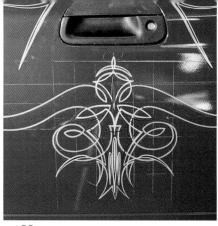

20

Step 19

At this point, I haven't removed the Stabilo lines because I want to add some silver as an accent color. Don't get too carried away with your design. Remember the old saying, "KISS"—keep it simple, stupid!

Step 20

I'm almost finished. As a final accent, I mix some of the silver with a few drops of black to create a charcoal color.

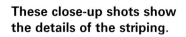

These close-up shots show the details of the striping.

Here's the completed pick-up truck in all its beauty!

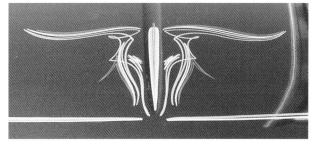

A Touch of Pinstriping Flair
Jimmy C

SUPPLIES

PAINT MEDIA: 1-Shot® Lettering Enamel
BRUSHES: #00, #2 Mack striping brushes, acid brush
OTHER: Grease pencil, baby powder

For hundreds of thousands of rodders, bikers, truckers, boaters, racers, and other vehicle enthusiasts, their machines aren't complete until they've been pin-striped. Sometimes it just takes a few pin lines of enamel down the side of a gal's PT Cruiser or on a few of the panels of a dude's Electraglide. Add a favorite color and now that boat or car is personal-ized. It's different—not the same as everyone else's! In the world of pinstriping, helping people make their vehicles original is a fun challenge. On a daily basis, you get to do something different. There's never a dull moment!

Pinstriping caught my attention when I was in my teens, living in a small town in southwestern Arizona. Soon after I bought my first van, I dreamt of customiz-ing it, but the only car shows I saw back then were the ones I read about in magazines. I saw cool rides all the time at work—I pumped gas for a few years. The cars were either coming from or going to California. Ever since I was a little kid listening to Wolfman Jack on the radio, I've been drawn to California—the Beach Boys, the ocean, surfing, girls, cars, bikes—all that!

In the late '60s and early '70s, although vans and Harley-Davidson sportsters were cool, custom ones were the coolest! My friends and I never missed the Internationals (drag races) at the Beeline Raceway outside of Phoenix. Bitchin'! The paint jobs on the cars just blew my mind! Color me gone! I didn't understand all the work that went into the finished product, but one thing was for sure—like so many kids then and now, I was captivated by those paint jobs. They got my attention and I loved them! It was-n't until I was 24 that I picked up a striping brush and started practicing all the time. I got a piece of glass to practice on and nobody's vehicle in the driveway was safe! I learned both brush control and self-confidence by painting signs on a daily basis.

Pinstriping and sign painting are different in a number of ways. First, they require different tools. A sword striping brush has a different feel than a lettering quill. Stripers are smaller and lighter, so you must have a lighter touch. Second, you have to con-centrate more when pinstriping, especially on long lines. It's what Von Dutch called "getting in the zone." Third, as a pinstriper, you have to be a contortionist! When striping, the only easy place to paint may be the hood or the deck. The rest of the time, you're standing on your head pulling the line by your nose and then stretching back out the other direction, all in one nonstop motion.

I enjoy pinstriping on just about anything, trash cans, mailboxes, cars, planes, cell phones—you name it! Panels are among my favorite things to pinstripe. Pinstriped panels evolved from sign painters and pinstripers who painted examples of their work on panels and then exchanged them. Soon they began collecting and trading panels at bashes, conventions, and reunions.

Although pinstriping has been around for thousands of years, it has only recently become a global craft.

But what's unique is that modern pinstriping is an American art form that has grown up with hot rodding. From there, interest spread among people from around the world who collect pinstriped goodies, not just because they're beautiful and colorful, but also because they're part of this American art form. The art of pinstriping is growing, and it's going to get a lot bigger before it goes away!

Well, that's my excuse for deciding to paint a canvas for this how-to section. I hope you enjoy it!

1

2

3

Step 1 *Pull Out a Canvas!*

You must coat your canvas before painting because pinstripes on "bare" canvas tend to bleed. I marbled this canvas with nearly every color in my box and then applied clearcoat, because the striping is going to be so big! Next, I gridded the canvas with a white grease pencil. When laying out and painting a large design, it's difficult to keep it uniform because you can't keep your eye on the side you just painted. The grid makes the layout easier and helps keep the design balanced.

Step 2 *Plan Your Design*

I don't usually do much preplanning, but I had a particular Tiki idea in my head that I wanted to work out. I wanted it to fit over the black line I already painted on the canvas.

Step 3 *Paper to Canvas*

I use the old string trick to make perfect arches in the Tiki's mouth. Boy, the grid really helps get the design uniform!

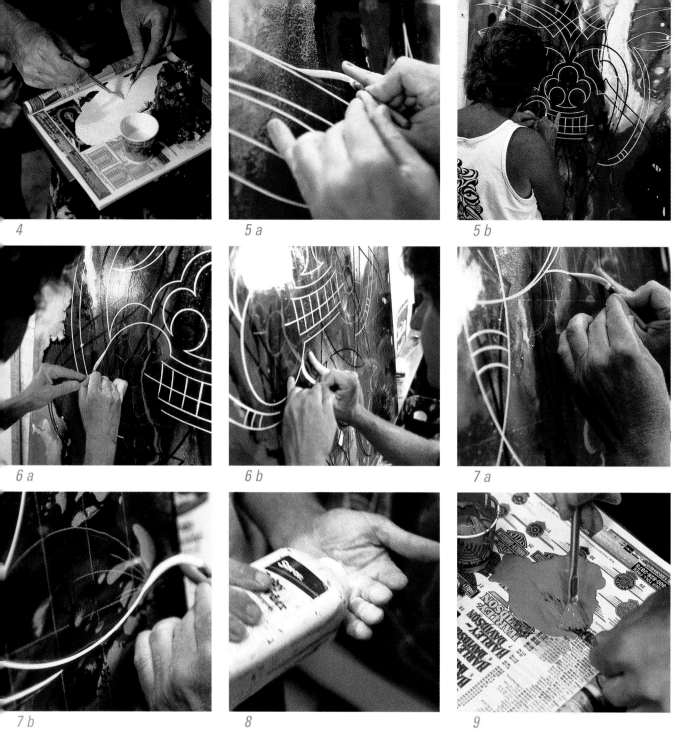

4

5 a

5 b

6 a

6 b

7 a

7 b

8

9

Step 4 *Palette!*

For this color, I mix up a light ivory. Because of the contrast, I choose a #00 brush for a thinner line. On the black, I use a #2 brush. I'll get back to paletting.

Step 5 *Start at the Top!*

I start at the top and work my way down. With something this big, it's easy to keep your hands out of the wet lines. When pulling a line, it's best to keep your eyes on where you're going, not on your brush. Look under your hand at your guideline.

Step 6 *Oh, Boy…Circles!*

To make circles, you have to twist the brush in the direction of the curve. Start at the top, twist all the way around to make the connection, and then come back from the top in the opposite direction to even out the line.

Step 7 *Overhand/Underhand*

Most lines I paint are overhand because I hold the brush using both hands. Here are examples of both overhand [7a] and underhand brushwork [7b].

Step 8 *Baby Powder?*

Yes, baby powder! Putting powder on your hands allows them to slide more smoothly. Also, powder comes in handy when matching pinstripes on an old faded job at a body shop where, for instance, a fender was replaced. A little powder mixed in with the paint makes it dry and dull, just like the old stripe you're matching!

Step 9 *Palette, Palette, Palette!*

I use an acid brush to load my striping brush. I got in the habit of using the acid brush to help me palette during the years I painted in the desert. Because the paint dried so quickly there, the acid brush helped keep my palette wet so it was less work on my striping brush. It is most definitely easier to stripe in cool weather than in hot!

Step 10 *Accents*

Accent colors can be a nice touch, but learning when to stop is a hard lesson. I choose yellow and green to match my background colors, not to contrast with them. The design is very simple, but looks like much more with the background colors and the metal flake. Now that's art!

10 a

10 b

10 c

Jimmy C

Tiki Blast-Off
Ettore "Blaster" Callegaro

SUPPLIES
PAINT MEDIA: 1-Shot® Lettering Enamel
BRUSHES: #00 Mack striping brush
OTHER: Synthetic thinner (to clean
brush and thin 1-Shot), Stabilo pencil

Ettore Callegaro, a.k.a. "Blaster," is a native of Chioggia, Italy, a small town near Venice. Since 1992, he has owned and operated a sign and decoration shop. Callegaro picked up his nickname nearly 20 years ago, when he started airbrushing and quickly became known for "blasting" color on any paintable surface he could find.

One of Italy's hottest pinstriping talents, Blaster takes you step-by-step through the creation of a Tiki-style spaceman, complete with his signature, intricate line work. Grab a brush and follow along.

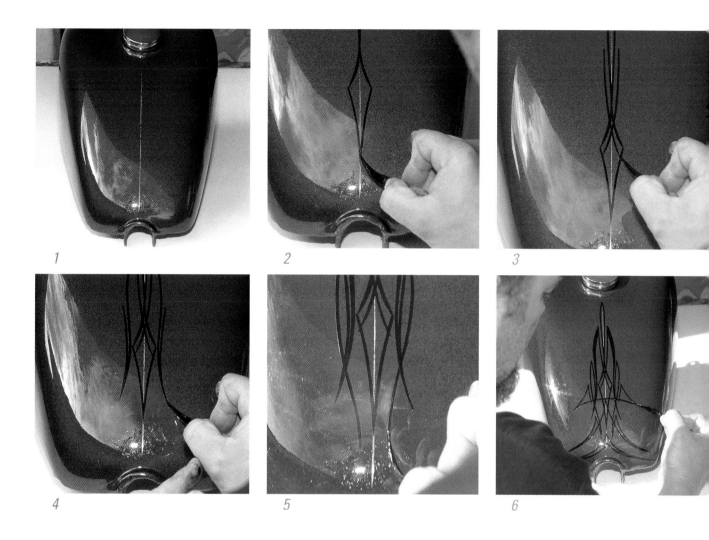

Step 1

To start, I always trace a middle line for balance with a Stabilo pencil. This helps me keep the striping vertical and symmetrical.

Step 2

I start with black straight from the can. To palette the paint, I squeeze it directly onto the glossy pages of a magazine, a paletting surface that's both cheap and easy to use. I palette the brush to load it with paint and then begin to make the first lines. Note: I never thin the paint. If needed, I dip the tip of the brush into a little thinner, then onto the palette to pick up the paint. Once my brush is loaded, I start with a central teardrop.

Step 3

I combine a series of concave and convex lines. I try hard to balance two things—my need to create symmetrical lines and my drive to follow my creative instincts.

Step 4

The pinstriping becomes more complex as the design develops.

Step 5

Now the design is really taking on a life of its own!

Step 6

Some "thick and thin" is cool here. I use this technique to add a bit of rhythm to the composition. It's much like music or architecture at this stage, in that we're going both for balance and tempo. At this point, this single-color pinstriping design could be ready for my signature, but I think it needs something more.

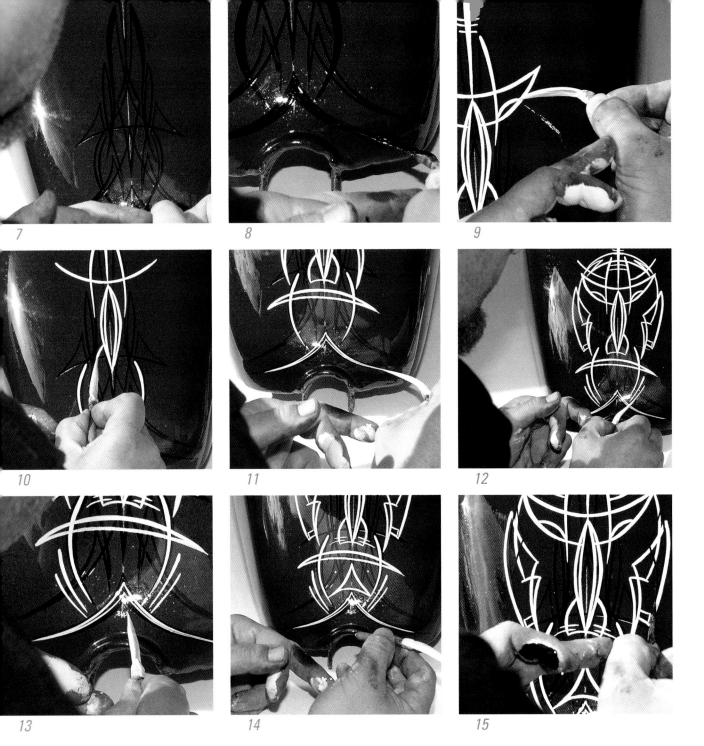

7

8

9

10

11

12

13

14

15

Step 7

I add more lines in white. Remember to clean the brush thoroughly before changing colors. White tends to get sticky before other colors do, especially on a hot summer day, so reduce it with a little thinner when needed.

Step 8

I always start with the left side of the design because I'm right-handed. This way, my hand won't block my view of the line I've just pulled. This also makes it easier to repeat the design on the right side of the pattern. Plus, I won't rub my hand against the wet paint on the left.

Step 9

I build up the face.

Step 10

I continue with the contour of the face. Note the rocket-style nose.

Step 11

I work on the mouth and the chin.

Step 12

I add more details to complete the face.

Step 13

Now I add my signature in white, using the same brush that I used for the entire pinstriping project. I hold the brush in reverse, working only with the point of the hairs. This allows me to sign my name with an ultra-skinny 3/32-inch line. People really flip out over this!

Step 14

I make dots with the end of the wooden brush handle. The cool part of using the handle is that the dots gradually become smaller as you use up the paint and are always perfectly round.

Step 15

I add more black over the white to provide contrast.

The Spaceman Tiki is ready to blast off! After letting the design dry overnight, I remove the pencil line with my fingers, and if necessary, some water. It's always a good idea to apply some nonabrasive wax to the design a few days later. I do not clear-coat my work, so a little wax helps protect the striping from the elements. Also, wax helps reduce the step between the pinstriping and the painted surface.

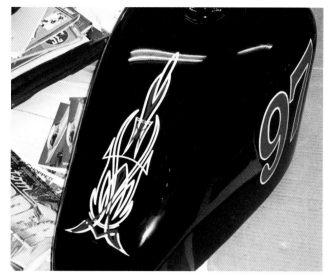

Striping Rat Fink

Coop

SUPPLIES

PAINT MEDIA: 1-Shot® Lettering Enamel
BRUSHES: Small liner or quill
OTHER: Stabilo pencil, Smoothie, mahl stick

In the early '70s, I bought my first van. Being the underpaid drone that I was, I customized the van myself. Learning by trial and error (mostly error), I finally made it look OK. In 1977, I got hooked up with a mural painter named Juan Parker, who put me to work striping in his shop. I got plenty of practice, but still wasn't sure what I was doing. No striper I ever met would tell me anything. One day I saw an article in a magazine about Ed "Big Daddy" Roth and the Rat Fink Reunion. Ed had a catalog of homemade books and videos about striping and lettering, so I excitedly sent away for these jewels. Sure enough, I learned a lot. When I needed answers, I would call Ed and he'd give me lots of help and inspiration.

Several years after I started, I realized that I needed to do more than just stripe, as I often got requests for lettering, graphics, and cartoons. I recommend learning these techniques to all beginning pinstripers. Not only will you make more money, but you won't have to tell the customer who wants a lettering job, "I can't do that." It just doesn't sound professional! Although lettering is akin to striping, you'll need to learn differ-

ent techniques. Pick a few lettering styles—block, script, bouncy freestyle brushstrokes—and master them. These have saved me more than once.

Another request I often get is for cartoon characters. They aren't complicated to do if you have good reference photos, and they make great additions to just about any car. Most people have a favorite character of some kind, so it's a good idea to have a collection of cartoons on hand to draw from. It's much easier to work from a drawing than to try to draw a character from memory. I like to carry coloring books for basic line art. Also, this lets customers look at poses and choose which ones they like.

One character that a lot of hot rodders like is Rat Fink™. For this how-to, I'll paint Rat Fink on a truck. The most beloved character of Ed Roth's cartoons, Finky has been one of Big Daddy's greatest legacies to the kustom industry. Finky is much more complicated than most cartoons, so good reference is very important.

  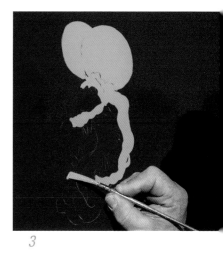

1   2   3

Step 1

Start by making sure your surface is clean. Next, sketch out the basic shape with a Stabilo pencil. Unlike a grease pencil, a Stabilo is water-soluble. Don't use a grease pencil or china marker; paint won't stick to either. Stabilos are available in several colors at art or sign supply shops. Try two or three different ones and find what you like. Be warned, however, that Stabilos get soft in warm weather. It helps to put them in a refrigerator or cooler just before using them.

I find it easier to get the proportions correct by drawing large basic shapes and dividing the design up from there. Make the sketch as accurate as possible—the initial shapes will be easier to paint in with color if they're as close as possible to the finished shape. Putting in some of the detail may help you get the shapes right, but don't spend too much time on details. The initial color will cover them up.

Step 2

When the sketch is finished, take a dry rag and lightly rub over the entire area. This will remove any heavy concentration of pencil. Leave just enough to see the image.

Step 3

Paint in the basic colors in the appropriate areas. "Fink Green" is a 50-50 mixture of 1-Shot Emerald Green and Lemon Yellow that results in a very bright lime green. You can mix a few drops of Smoothie fish-eye eliminator with the paint. It will help the paint flow out, giving it more gloss and preventing fish-eyes caused by any foreign substance you might have missed on your surface (I've even had fish-eyes caused by kerosene space heaters, so it's a good idea always to use Smoothie).

It's helpful to leave shapes within colored areas so you can see where detail lines should go. Don't paint areas solid if you have underlying details to add. If you use the Smoothie, you'll have to use it in all of your paint, otherwise the "non-Smoothied" paint may fish-eye or react with the Smoothie-treated paint.

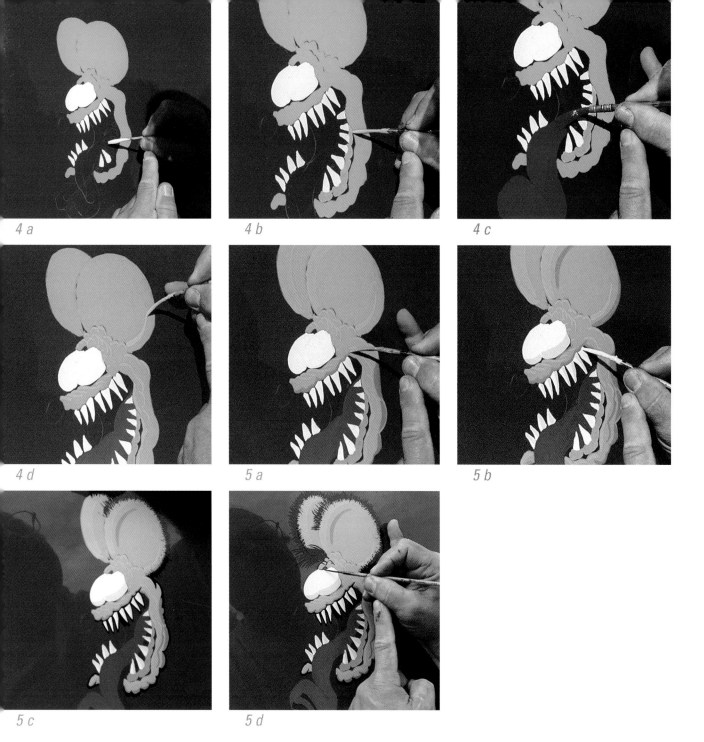

4 a

4 b

4 c

4 d

5 a

5 b

5 c

5 d

Step 4

After letting the base colors dry for a few minutes, shadow the areas with lighter and darker colors. Mix a little green to create a darker shade of Fink Green. Work underside areas away from the light source to give "shape" to your cartoon. To shade white areas, use a few drops of blue in white. This gives the teeth and eyes a nice shadow. Next, brush a lighter shade on the high areas toward the light source.

I suggest letting this dry as much as possible before painting the black detail—if the base colors are wet, the paints will run together. Also, if you make a mistake, you can wipe it off without spoiling what you've already done.

Step 5

I like to use a small liner to add detail, but a small quill also works nicely. Carefully draw detail working from left to right (reverse this if you're left-handed). This helps keep your fingers out of the wet paint. Another technique is to use a mahl stick, a round stick with a soft ball or cork on one end to rest your hand on over wet paint. Some people use them all the time; others rarely use them. Try it to see if you like it. You can make a good mahl stick by attaching a wine cork to a dowel rod.

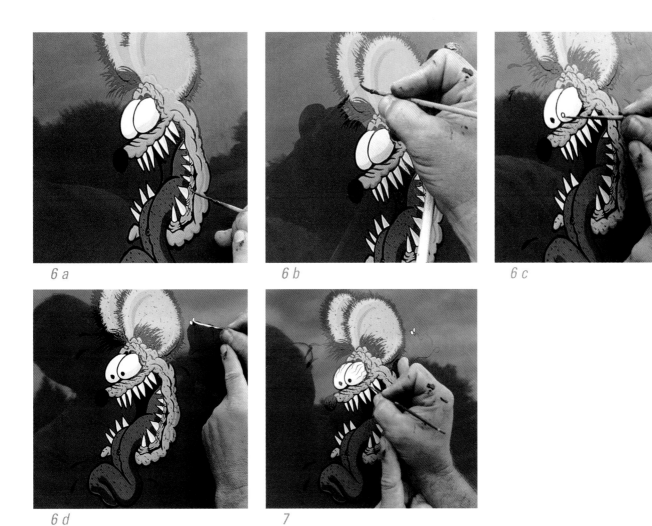

6 a

6 b

6 c

6 d

7

Step 6

A cartoon should have a heavy black outline to make it stand out. Remember to put Smoothie in your paint whenever the base colors have Smoothie in them. If you don't, your black will fish-eye.

Step 7

Finish off your cartoon with red in the eyes. On a black vehicle, the outline should be dark gray; otherwise it will disappear against the background. If you make a mistake, you can clean it up with a rag wrapped over the end of your brush handle.

TIPS FROM COOP

1 I've noticed that nearly all the stripers I've met hold their brushes a little bit differently. There is no one "proper" way to hold your brush. Whatever is comfortable for you is the right way. With practice and repetition you'll learn to manipulate the brush.

2 When working on a fresh paint job, use a low-tack tape for a guide or masking. Be very careful to pull off the masking tape back over itself slowly. It's no fun trying to explain to a customer why a big hunk of his paint job is missing!

3 Some colors that aren't used often can get thick or lumpy. If this happens, pour the paint through a strainer or a piece of pantyhose nylon.

4 1-Shot now has a catalyst and hardener for 1-Shot lettering enamels. It's pretty effective at increasing the paint's adhesion and helping it hold its gloss longer. I like to use it like thinner, mixing it in the brush as I dip between strokes. The directions will tell you to mix it 50-50, but I find this thins the paint too much.

5 Don't work on a car in the sun. It may be difficult if you're working at a car show or if your customer doesn't have a place inside, but be warned that a car in the sun will get hot enough to put blisters on your fingers. The paint will dry as soon as it hits the surface. The glue on the tape will melt and stay on the car, causing a mess. The wind also can be a big problem, so try to get some cover. Bugs also pose a challenge. If you get a bug in the paint and it smears, fix it right away.

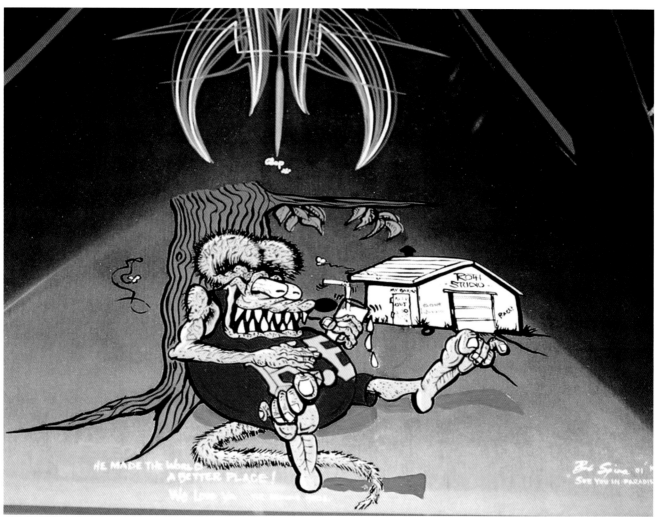

Willis Dormer

SUPPLIES

BRUSH: #0 Mack Series 10 brushes
PAINT MEDIA: 1-Shot® Lettering Enamel
OTHER: 5-Star wax and grease remover,
#12 pounce wheel, 220-grit dry
sandpaper

Californian Willis Dormer has been pinstriping since 1975. In the past three decades, he has done professional lettering, sign painting, and T-shirt airbrushing, in addition to his pinstripe work. Follow along as Willis flames out a Nissan Frontier.

1

2 a

2 b

Step 1

For the best results, make sure you start with a clean surface. The first thing I do is prep the truck with a wax and grease remover—5-Star is my brand of choice. Wearing rubber gloves, I wipe down all areas that I plan to stripe. While the solvent is still wet, I wipe it off with a clean dry rag. Wiping the area with a slightly damp rag will eliminate any static electricity.

Step 2

I draw my flame layout on paper, which I tape to the truck. Starting on the hood, I sketch the flames from center, going left onto the fender working back to the door. After a few changes in the pencil sketch, things can get a little confusing, so I go over the flames with a more precise outline using a Sharpie marker.

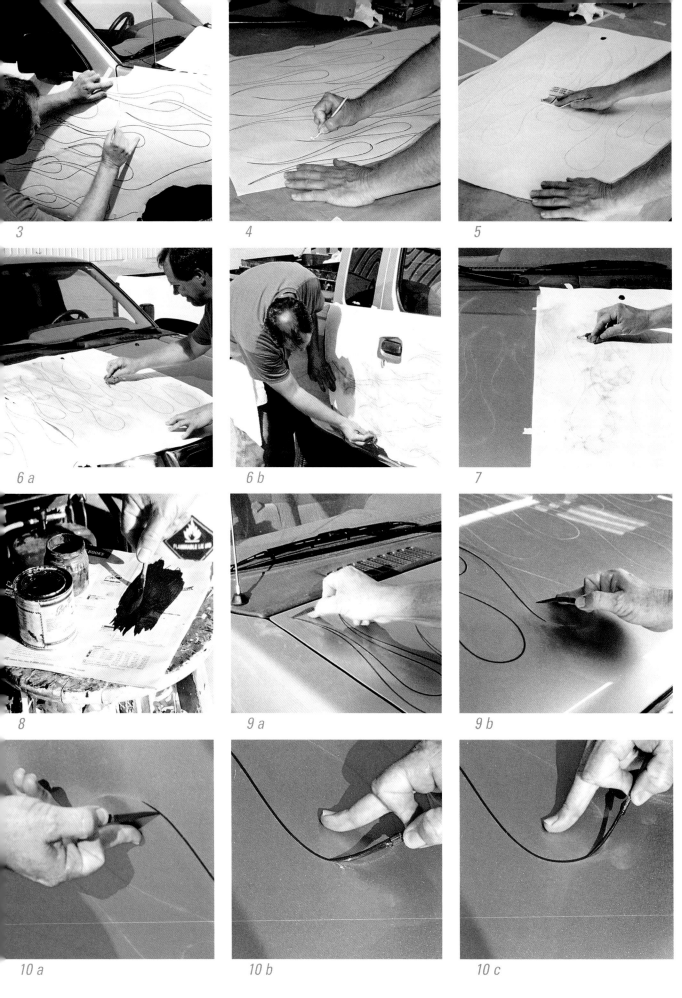

3

4

5

6 a

6 b

7

8

9 a

9 b

10 a

10 b

10 c

Step 3

The side paper is one long piece, so I cut it into three pieces at the doorjambs using an X-Acto knife.

Step 4

I perforate holes by tracing the pattern with a #12 pounce wheel. I use three layers of masking paper to get a soft underside, and I apply a fair amount of pressure as the wheel rolls along.

Step 5

Turning the pattern over, I sand off the perforation using 220-grit dry sandpaper.

Step 6

I tape the patterns to the truck and using a blue pounce bag, I rub along the design, patting a little as I go.

Step 7

I turn the pattern over and pounce it, leaving an identical flamed pattern from the center of the hood going right. I repeat the process on the driver's side of the truck.

Step 8

Now I thin some 1-Shot Proper Purple with paint thinner. The brush I'm using is a #0 Mack Series 10. I like to use magazines to palette and mix my paint. I dip the brush into the paint and put the paint onto the magazine. Then I dip the brush into the jar of thinner and mix it with the paint until it feels right. The paint-to-thinner ratio varies between 3:1 and 5:1.

Step 9

I start on the hood working from left to right. I pull the line from the tip of the flame, stopping as I approach the turn. I'm right-handed, so working from left to right keeps my finger from smearing the work. Guiding your brush with only one finger down, not two or three, will help you smear less.

Step 10

Starting the turn, I put the tip down 3/4-inch back on the line and using my middle finger, I pivot through the turn.

Step 11

My turn is a little easier as I get to the right side, because I can stand on the side of the truck. If I had striped the sides first, I would risk smearing the work.

Step 12

You can make corrections with your finger, a cloth towel, or heavy-duty paper. You should only wash cloth towels once or twice when using them on your surface to reduce the amount of lint that could stick to the stripe. In doing the repair, load your brush with less paint. This makes the touch-up easier to control.

Step 13

Starting from the tip, I pull the right side of the flame back into the turn.

11

12

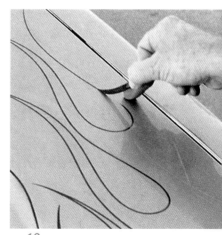

13

14

15

16

17

18

19

20

21

22

23

24 a

24 b

Step 14

You can stripe either side of the truck next. On the passenger side, I start at the front, working along the top towards the back.

Step 15

I leave an opening for the tip of the red middle flames to cross over.

Step 16

I put the top line leading into each tip on first. Next, I do my turn.

Step 17

I can't pivot here, so I use two hands to steady myself through the turn. I slowly twist the brush to the right during the turn to help me get a consistent line.

Step 18

I pick up the line at the top of the turn and pull the lower flame line into the tip. Next I pick up from the bottom of the turn and pull to the next tip.

Step 19

Once I reach the back flame, I work forward along the bottom.

Step 20

I bring this turn forward and stop it where another crossover flame comes in. I then pull the bottom line in the turn to the tip.

Step 21

Starting from the front turn, I pull the bottom line into the tip. Then I pick up the line under the crossover and pull back to the tip again.

Step 22

I stripe the middle or inside flame with 1-Shot Bright Red. Using the same steps as the purple flames, I work along the top to the back and then along the bottom, moving forward. Coming to a crossover, I stop just shy of the wet purple line. Remember: top line, turn, bottom line.

Step 23

I put my finger on the other side of the purple turn, touch down, and finish the tip.

Step 24

Being comfortable is important, so I'm sitting on a stepstool as I stripe this turn, but for the long lines, I bend over.

Step 25

Coming to the tips, I pull away from the truck while still in motion to get pointed tips.

Step 26

On the driver's side, I start at the front, pulling from the tip to the turn, then I move back one step at a time.

24 c

25

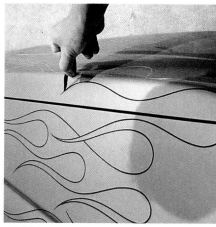

26

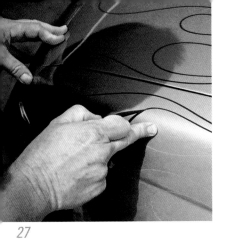

27   28   29

30

Step 27

I do this turn with the same pivoting motion I used on the hood.

Step 28

From the tip though the turn, you can do this entire part in one motion with practice.

Step 29

My left hand gives me support, but I am careful not to touch any wet stripes.

Step 30

Straying from your chalk mark a little throughout the job is OK, except when connecting your line at the turns.

Here is the finished job. You can take off any chalk marks with a damp rag after the paint dries. In warm weather, your dry time will be between 1 and 3 hours, and in cold weather, drying will take between 2 and 8 hours.

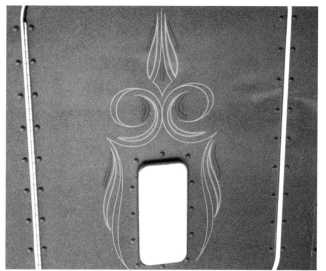

Willis Dormer

COLO. PUC 6614 I
COLO. GTM-80-21821
IOWA CC 49349

Bobbo Dunn

SUPPLIES

PAINT MEDIA: 1-Shot® Lettering Enamel
BRUSHES: Lavallee brushes by Mack
OTHER: 3M™ Fine Line masking tape (#215)

In 1947, 13-year-old Bobbo Dunn won a scholarship from General Motors for building a clay model. Bobbo never used the scholarship, but he soon entered the signage and lettering trade in his home-town of Visalia, California. He got some of his first work through a bowling alley, where he worked setting up pins. Bobbo's talent was put to use in lettering and painting 3-D artwork on customers' bowling bags. At age 17, he enlisted in the army, working as a graphic artist until he was sent to fight in the Korean War. After being transferred from the front line, Bobbo set up one of the first military sign shops in Korea. He continued doing sign work for the military in San Francisco after he was rotated back to the States.

When Kenneth "Von Dutch" Howard pioneered the striping craze in the 1950s and '60s, Bobbo jumped on the bandwagon and found he was a natural at flame painting. Bobbo became a regular at racing events and car shows, where he painted and lettered numerous dragsters and racecars of all sorts. Bobbo was one of the original founding fathers of the kus-tom hot rod industry. Other kustom painters, such as

Ed Roth, Von Dutch, Larry Watson, Dean Jeffries, Tom Kelly, and George and Sam Barris, were Bobbo's con-temporaries and friends.

Bobbo's artwork has been a constant inspiration to pinstripers and airbrushers alike. Now at an age when most professionals think of retirement, Bobbo is still going strong. In the last decade, he has been published by just about every automotive magazine out there. *Airbrush Action, Autographics, Auto Art, Sign Business,* and *Truckin'* have showcased his work for years. Like all the great kustom auto artists, Bobbo's work continues to evolve with kustom industry.

Since his move to Albuquerque, New Mexico, Bobbo has been known for his new hybrid work with a Southwestern spin. Modifying existing American Indian art styles, Bobbo has created some fantastic panel work and automotive custom paint jobs that contain both of these truly American influences. In the following demo, Bobbo shows you one of his hybrid Southwestern designs.

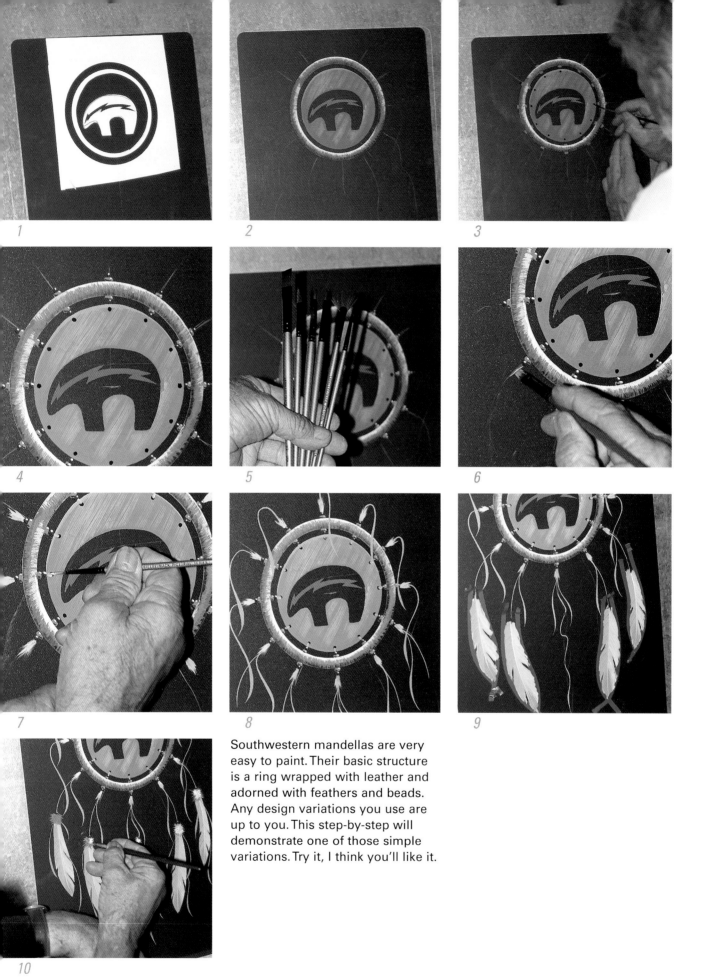

1

2

3

4

5

6

7

8

9

Southwestern mandellas are very easy to paint. Their basic structure is a ring wrapped with leather and adorned with feathers and beads. Any design variations you use are up to you. This step-by-step will demonstrate one of those simple variations. Try it, I think you'll like it.

10

Step 1

I first lay out the panel with a center line, then cut a mask for a good circle. I computer-cut this sample to get a perfect edge.

Step 2

The first color I lay in is tan; then I add shadows in brown, highlights in white, and a few streaks in the bear circle. I will try to make it look like a wrapped leather ring with a flat leather circle and a bear painted on it.

Step 3

Next, I lay out 12 equal points and paint in the beads and black dots to represent holes for holding the center leather circle onto the ring.

Step 4

This close-up shows the painted beads with shadows and highlights and the black dots with the orange lightning bolt in the bear.

Step 5

To paint the feathers and the down, I use my Lavallee brushes by Mack.

Step 6

I paint the leather strips that tie the bear circle to the ring and the feathers, which are used for ornamentation.

Step 7

At this point, I render the connecting leather strips and their highlights.

Step 8

To create a nice balanced design, I paint in some random leather strips.

Step 9

I use 3M™ Fine Line masking tape to shape the feathers. When I have the shape I want, I then paint it in. I use a 1/2-inch Lavallee brush to shape them in color, and then I unmask the tape.

Step 10

When painting the down, I first lay down pink, then layer white over it. Using a 1/4-inch flat Lavallee brush, blend the white and pink to bleed the colors for different shades.

Step 11

Here is the completed piece—a perfect example of Old World folk art modernized for today's pinstriping and automotive market, proving that hot rod pinstriping is not just about eyeballs and flaming dice!

Bobbo Dunn

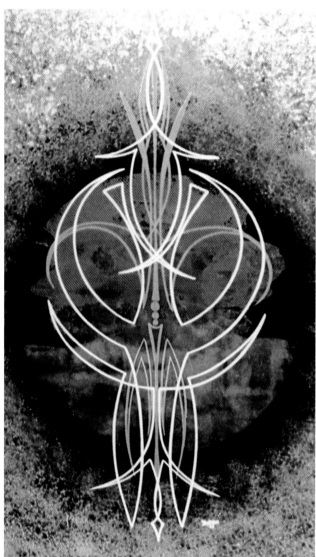

Bobbo Dunn

Waking the Dead

E-Dog

SUPPLIES

PAINT MEDIA: 1-Shot® Lettering Enamel,
House of Kolor urethane paints
BRUSHES: Mack striping brushes,
Sata NR2000 spray gun
OTHER: Air-powered grinder

While working in a diesel trailer assembly plant,
California pinstriper E-Dog learned to use a spray
gun, then developed a wider interest in art after
rooming with several talented artists. At the time E-
Dog thought his drawing skills were lacking, so he
learned to express himself with a different kind of art
form—modern pinstriping. Like so many others in his
field, E-Dog lacks formal art education and is self-
taught. He was inspired to begin pinstriping in 1996
after seeing some awesome paint jobs at car shows.
Working out of his garage in Riverside, E-Dog stays
busy with projects on cars, motorcycles, bikes, aluminum panels, oil drums, and retro '50s furniture.
Many of his early and current influences in the hot
rod kulture are Maxx Gramajo, Jeff Soto, BMV, Jon
Chase, and such legends as Jimmy Cleveland, Daddy-
O, Japanese pinstriper Makoto, Enamel and Mr. G,
and the late Ed "Big Daddy" Roth.

1   2   3

4   5   6

Step 1

For this job, E-Dog got his hands on an aluminum casket. There's nothing nicer than a little Kandy painting and some striping to give a casket that cheery look.

Step 2

Using an air-powered grinder, E-Dog creates a series of vertical stripes in the aluminum. You'll see how nicely the automotive Kandy plays off of this texture. Use a low-grit grinding pad so you don't leave too deep a mark, just enough for the effect.

Step 3

You can see the grinding pattern in the sun when the job is finished. Now E wipes down the aluminum with soap and water or a little alcohol. Never use precleaner on aluminum—it will damage the surface and cause the paint to delaminate from the aluminum base.

Step 4

Adding some House of Kolor Kandy Tangerine Koncentrate to SG-100 intercoat clear, E-Dog pours the mixture into his spray gun in preparation for the painting. Be sure never to add more than 20% Kandy Koncentrate to the SG-100, otherwise the Kandy may not lock into the clear and could reactivate later.

Step 5

E-Dog uses a gravity-feed spray gun to layer the kandy over the aluminum in even vertical passes, mimicking the vertical pattern of the grinder.

Step 6

Adding some gold ice pearl to the SG-100, E-Dog gets ready to spray a protective layer of clear over the entire job. This added coat of clear will make the ice pearl pop out. It also protects the Kandy.

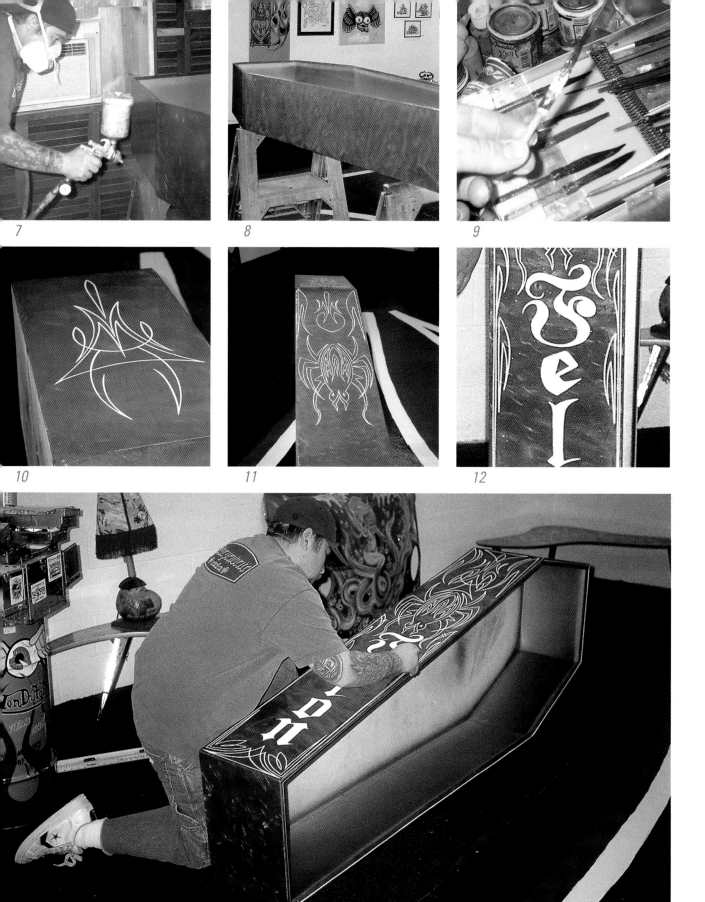

7

8

9

10

11

12

13

Step 7

A few good wet coats of intercoat clear brighten up the Kandy in the light.

Step 8

It's a good idea to let the intercoat and underlying Kandy coats cure for an hour or so before striping. If the coats are too fresh, the striping may reactivate the color, causing it to bleed into the striping.

Step 9

Going through his great collection of oiled brushes, E-Dog selects a Mack sword striper to begin pinstriping.

Step 10

Using only a single center line as a guide, E-Dog begins striping with some symmetrical patterning. This is on the top bevel side of the casket. Notice how well the 1-Shot white punches out from the Kandy Tangerine background.

Step 11

Working down the long side of the casket, E-Dog continues striping in the same style. What casket would be complete without a spider?

Step 12

A little lettering balances out the whole design. Of course, it's not hot rod lettering unless you can't decipher it!

Step 13

Using the same white and his sword striper, E-Dog borders the entire design, including the lettering.

And there you have the finished product, E-Dog and all. The hot rod casket fits right into E-Dog's newest gallery and hot rod store, 3 Deuces.

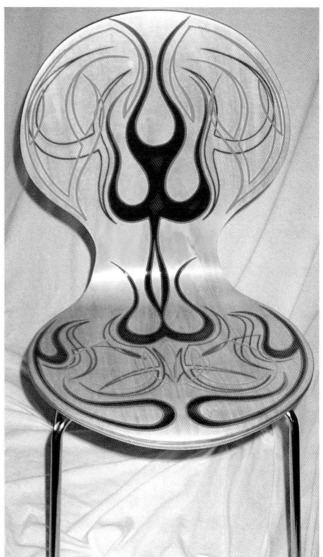

Pinstriping with a Beugler
Don Edwards

SUPPLIES

PAINT MEDIA: 1-Shot® Lettering Enamel
BRUSHES: Xcaliber brush
OTHER: Kraft paper, pounce wheel and pad,
sandpaper, Beugler striping wheel,
magnetic guide strip, masking tape,
yard stick

About 30 years ago, while attending a car show, I saw a guy demonstrating a striping tool called a "Beugler." He made this tool look so easy to operate that I just had to have one. It came in two varieties—the deluxe kit with three wheel heads and the professional kit with six wheel heads. I quickly parted with my money and rushed home to try it. After only a few minutes, I realized that this tool was not going to be easy to master.

It took persistence, but over the years, I got pretty quick at laying down straight lines with the magnetic tape. I gradually started using the Beugler in some of my scrollwork on transports where the patterns were large. I would paint all the long sections with the Beugler and all the turns and flairs with a sword brush.

Today, I own four Beuglers and use them for all my striping, from straight lines to scrolls to outlining flames and graphics. Although traditionalists still consider using this tool to be cheating, if you stripe large scroll patterns (or just don't like refilling your brush while standing on a ladder), give the Beugler a try. You won't learn overnight, but in time you will find it to be a valuable tool in your striping kit.

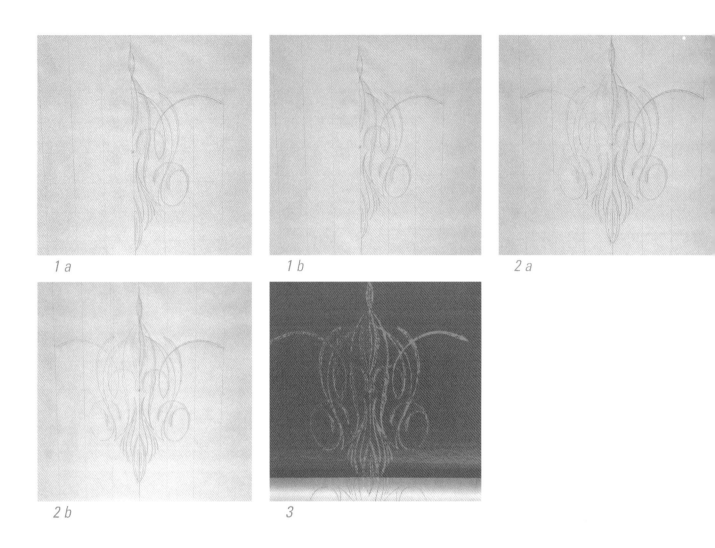

1 a

1 b

2 a

2 b

3

Step 1 *Create a Pattern*

Using kraft paper, draw a center line and freehand half of a scroll pattern with a pencil. You can create a grid pattern to help with design balance. Working on a soft background (like rubber or soft wood), I perforate holes along half the design with a pounce wheel.

Step 2 *Pouncing*

Fold the pattern along the center line so the back of the pounced side is now facing you. Lightly sand the paper to open the holes made by the pounce wheel. Take a pounce bag and rub it across the perforated holes. (You can make a pounce bag with powdered charcoal in an old T-shirt or even construction chalk in a sock.). Next, reopen the paper and use the pounce wheel on the other half of the design. You can use the imprint left from the first side as your guide. When this side is finished, sand the whole back. Now you are ready to apply the pattern to your project surface.

Step 3 *Transferring*

First, wipe the surface with a damp cloth and then degrease it. Next, tape the pattern in place. Draw a center line on the project surface and line it up to the pattern's center line. Rub the pounce bag across the pattern to transfer it to the project surface. Blow off any excess powder—too much of it will affect your striping.

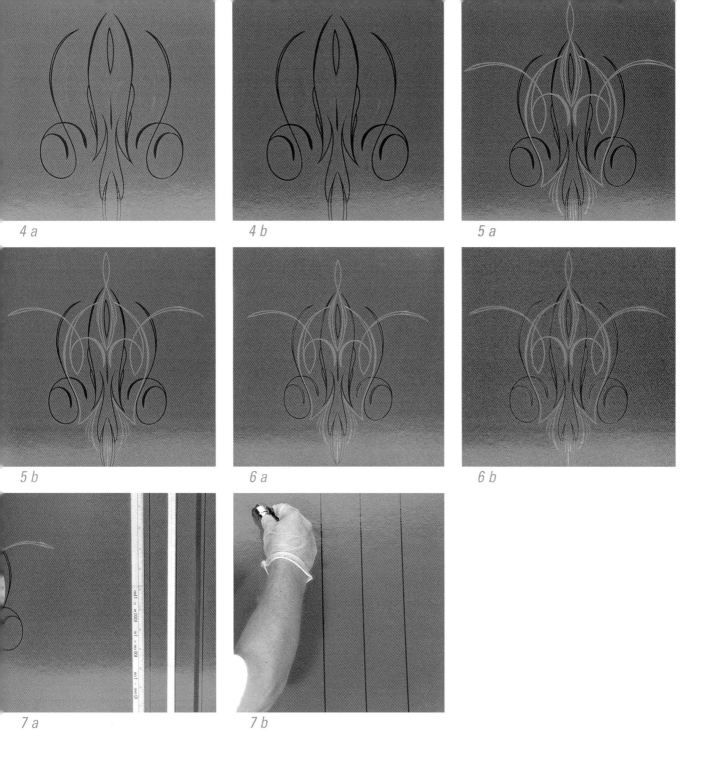

4 a

4 b

5 a

5 b

6 a

6 b

7 a

7 b

Step 4 *Enter Beugler*

Load the Beugler with un-thinned 1-Shot enamel. Prime the tube by pushing the plunger up until you see paint peeking out of the top by the wheel. Run the wheel across a palette (the surface of an old magazine or phone book will work) to start the paint. You must do this every time you start a new line or change directions, otherwise the line will have a skip at the beginning. Start the wheel on its edge and slowly straighten up to continue the line. Finish the line by rolling the Beugler back on its edge again. Tip: To hold the Beugler properly, think of it as a striping brush, not as a pencil.

Step 5 *Second Color*

Wait until the first color has dried, then apply the second color using the same method. Use a sword brush to create the thick flairs or to turn the corners if you have trouble doing this with the Beugler.

Step 6 *Highlights*

I have added a highlight to the thick sections of the stripe by taking the original color and adding some white to it. You may also darken the sections using black or purple added to the original color. Load up the sword brush and slowly pull up to create a point to the line, pushing down as you start.

Step 7 *Making Straight Lines*

The Beugler comes with three guides that fit in the top of the tube to help you create straight lines. The most popular is the magnetic strip. After making sure it's straight, set the guide up against the magnetic strip and work backward along the vehicle. Use your thumb to make sure the guide stays tight to the strip. The wheel of the Beugler will track away from the strip if you do not keep the two parallel.

You can also use a yardstick for painting short lines on nonmetallic surfaces. Either hold it or tape it in place. Another method is a body crease, which is the trickiest to keep parallel. Place a piece of tape at the end of the guide so that you don't mark the surface of the vehicle. If none of these methods work for you, you can use a tape guide (masking tape), but you cannot use the Beugler guide for this—it cannot track along small edges like tape. Use your index finger to track along the edge of the tape, and the line will stay parallel to the tape.

You should practice starting and stopping the Beugler, twisting the barrel as you go. Remember to keep the barrel perpendicular to the surface to keep the line consistent.

Beuglers are available in two sizes—the larger one comes with the kits. The kit also contains three guides, three or six heads in various sizes, and a cleaning brush. A magnetic strip is a must for long stripes. A dual head with equal and unequal heads is available, but it only works on perfectly flat surfaces.

TIPS FOR USING A BUEGLER

Never use thinned 1-Shot paint. Thinning the paint makes it too runny, and you won't get a clean line. You may also have the same problem with adding catalyst to the paint.

Because a Beugler is harder to clean than a brush, try to keep two of them on hand. This allows you to do a standard two-color stripe while out of the shop without having to worry about cleaning the striper until you return to the shop.

Cleaning can be done by soaking the parts in a tin of mineral spirits or running them under a parts cleaner.

Oil all parts with brush oil after cleaning.

Using a brush to finish lines or turns must be done immediately after using the Beugler to prevent the stripe from setting and drying unevenly.

Pre-roll striper on palette to prevent skipping at the beginning of the line due to dry paint on the wheel.

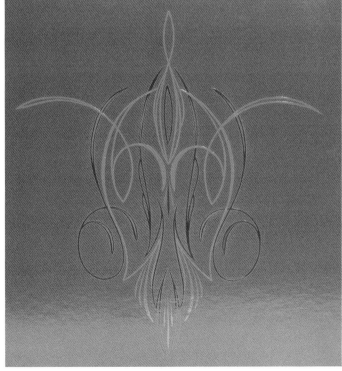

Don Edwards

Kustom PT Kruiser

Enamel

SUPPLIES

PAINT MEDIA: 1-Shot® Lettering Enamel
BRUSHES: #000 Mack striping brush
OTHER: Reducer, water-based greased pencil

Enamel was born in Iwaki City in Fukushima, Japan, in 1966. Inspired by the work of Ed "Big Daddy" Roth, Enamel began his pinstriping career in 1990. He made his U.S. debut in 1998 at the Rat Fink Reunion, and since then, he has been recognized as one of the world's foremost pinstripers. At the 1999 Yokohama Hot Rod Custom Show, he was named Speed King after winning the show's pinstriping race. Since then, his appearances have included the Cruisin' Nationals 1999-2002 in Paso Robles, California, the Rat Fink Reunion 1999, and Tokyo Groovy 2000 and 2001. Follow along with Japanese line master Enamel as he pinstripes this PT Cruiser.

Photos by Tomoaki "Nack" Nakura

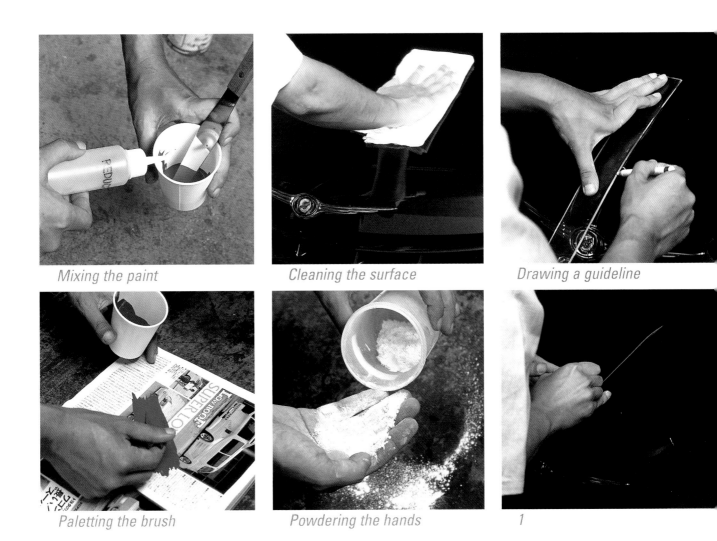

Mixing the paint

Cleaning the surface

Drawing a guideline

Paletting the brush

Powdering the hands

1

Prep

To prepare for his striping work, Enamel mixes 1-Shot Process Blue with reducer. Then he cleans the surface of the PT Cruiser with wax and grease remover to eliminate any dust and grime.

Next, Enamel draws his center guideline with a water-based grease pencil and palettes his brush with the Process Blue.

Enamel applies powder to his hands to help them slide over his striping surface more easily.

Step 1

Using his sword striper, Enamel lays down his center line.

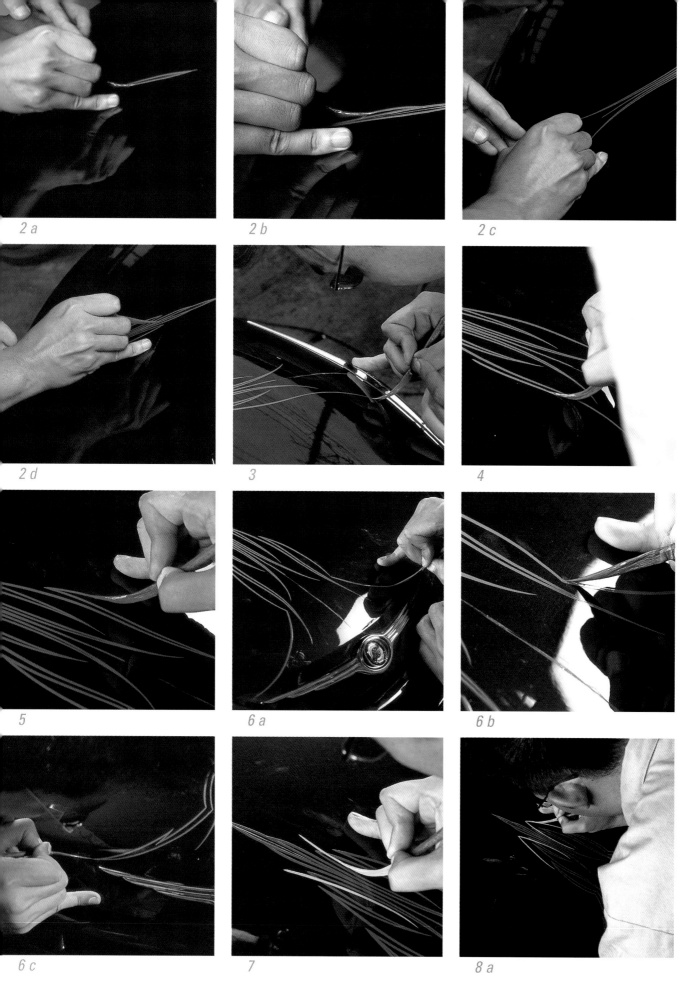

2 a

2 b

2 c

2 d

3

4

5

6 a

6 b

6 c

7

8 a

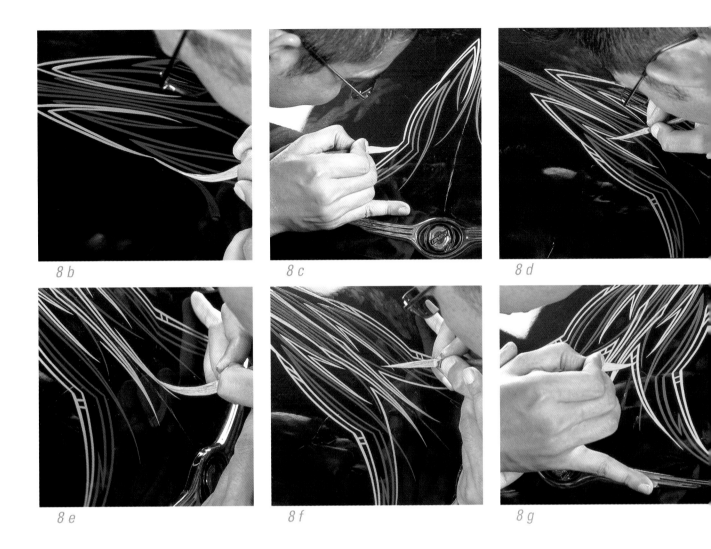

8 b   8 c   8 d

8 e   8 f   8 g

Step 2

As the line develops, Enamel works back and forth, starting with the left side of the design and then moving on to the right side.

Step 3

Enamel continues to build up his design, balancing his right hand on top of his left hand for maximum support.

Step 4

Still using the Process Blue, Enamel expands his design, paying close attention to symmetry and balance.

Step 5

Enamel completes the outside of the line.

Step 6

Next, he wraps up the Process Blue with a long, curved line.

Step 7

Next, Enamel uses Peacock Blue, the second and final color in this design.

Step 8

The design unfolds as Enamel uses the Peacock Blue to complete his pinstriped masterpiece.

Step 9

For the final step, Enamel adds his signature.

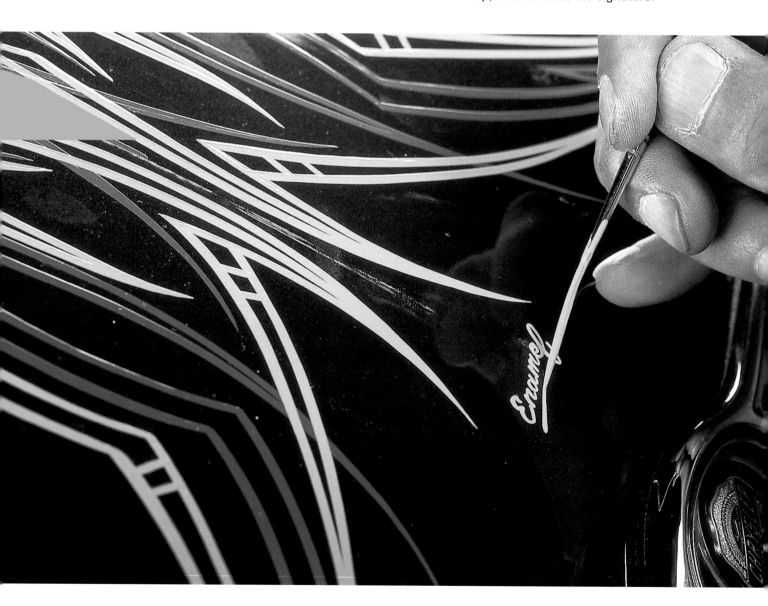

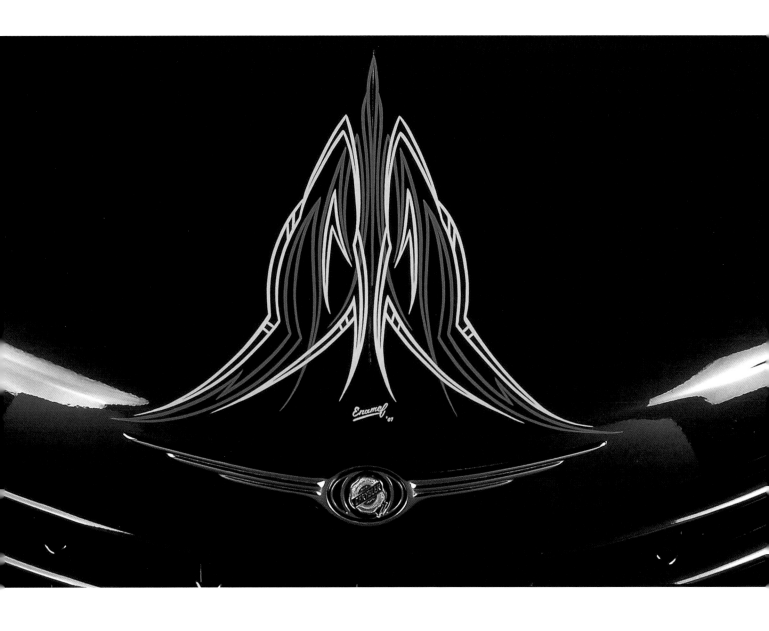

Enamel

Daddy-O Designs
Willy Fisher

SUPPLIES

PAINT MEDIA: 1-Shot® Lettering Enamel
BRUSHES: #00 Mack brush
OTHER: Mahl stick, masking tape, yard stick

Known in the kustom kulture world as Daddy-O, Willy Fisher is famous for his old school airbrush and pin-stripe work, especially his artistic hot rod cutouts and wall hangings. If there was a car show or trucking event in the 1970s or '80s, odds were that Willy would be there with his one-man traveling airbrush act, going by the name "Gemini." Renowned both for his artistic creations on T-shirts and his speedy painting, Willy has reinvented his style countless times while maintaining the quality that made him famous.

1 2 3
4 5 6

Step 1

To be a little different, Willy decided to do his pinstriping demo on a pizza pan, which is a perfect canvas; it doesn't need a frame and the brushed aluminum surface provides a good contrast to the pinstriping. Starting out with black 1-Shot, Willy palettes the #00 Mack brush on a phone book to work the paint into the bristles. Working from the center out, Willy starts laying out his symmetrical design.

Step 2

As he expands the design, you can see how he uses the mahl stick to keep his hand from dragging on the wet paint. Using the mahl stick is a skill that comes with practice, but as many sign painters will tell you, once you have mastered it, it is difficult to work without one.

Step 3

Willy works on balancing the design by first extending the pattern on the left and then mimicking it on the right. This prevents his brush hand from blocking his view of the artwork he is trying to copy (lefties should do the opposite).

Step 4

You can see the advantage of the mahl stick in allowing you to raise and lower your support surface to get the best brush angle.

Step 5

Using the tip of the brush, Willy can achieve incredibly thin and even line work. A well-trimmed sword striper also results in needle-sharp end points.

Step 6

As you work the design to the outside edge of the pan, it is important to keep an eye on balance. The further the design spreads, the easier it is to make balance mistakes when you are mimicking each side.

7

8

9

10

11

Step 7

The fun part about pinstriping is that there isn't always a great difference between steps, especially when dealing with a two-color design. Willy continues expanding the design to fill the pie pan.

Step 8

Centering up the design with his brush, Willy is eyeballing his progress, making sure the design is properly balanced.

Step 9

Another benefit of working on the pan is that you can spin it around as needed, not something you can do easily with a car! You can also see how Willy has used varying line thickness to break up the all-black design.

Step 10

With the black design finished, Willy switches to red. Starting from the center, he continues the design work. It is important to clean out the brush completely when switching colors, because a trace amount of black can radically darken the value of the red.

Step 11

Working his way out to the edge, Willy crisscrosses his original design and fills in the remaining area of the pan. In many ways, a two-color design is more difficult to paint than a multicolor design, but remember, less is more.

Notice the use of the varied line thickness in both the red and black designs in the finished piece. This makes the artwork more interesting and gives the eye points of focus. When all the lines are of equal thickness, the design often looks too busy and cluttered. This pan is an excellent example of minimalist kustom painting in the true old school tradition!

SOME WORDS FROM DADDY-O...

When people ask me how long I have been striping, my usual answer is "all day." But seriously, I have been pinstriping for just a few years, and only recently have I taken it seriously. I like to use a mahl stick for pinstriping because of my extensive lettering and sign painting work through the years. It helps keep my hands out of the wet paint. I don't need to let the paint dry to finish a piece—I just find a dry spot, put the stick there, and go for it. This is important since I primarily use 1-Shot lettering enamel, which takes a while to dry. In spite of this, I have always used 1-Shot and probably always will. My brush of choice is currently a #00 Mack sword striper. My art nowadays is mostly brushwork and less airbrushing. Pinstriping is a great way to add a cool look to my new work. Some of my recent work is just pinstripe designs with graphics—no airbrushing at all. My favorite things to paint are 1950s-style hood designs and old school graphics, usually short curved line designs, and no hoop-d-do's.

The first time I saw someone pinstripe was in the late 1950s at a body shop where my Dad worked. The striper, who was really a sign painter by trade, worked under the name "Rembrandt Signs," and instead of using a brush, he used a roller from J.C. Whitney. When I was about 9 years old, Rembrandt put a gold pinstripe around the bodylines of Dad's '36 Ford. I got to try pinstriping that day—he let me stripe the toolbox. I don't know if they left it there, they might have wiped it off, but I got to try out the roller. A few years later, Dad brought home a Mack brush from the auto supply shop. He asked me to put the numbers on our family boat. They looked terrible, but Dad left them on anyway. In the next year, I saw lots of striping at car shows and at school, but everybody else's work looked so good that I didn't give it another chance until I started painting motorcycles in 1971. It took a lot of work before I felt comfortable with my striping.

Willy Fisher

Willy Fisher

Hot Rod Stripin'
Craig Fraser

SUPPLIES

PAINT MEDIA: House of Kolor urethane paints
BRUSHES: Lettering quill, Xcaliber sword striper,
Iwata RG-3 spray gun, Iwata Eclipse airbrush
OTHER: Red Scotch-Brite® pad, precleaner,
3M™ Fine Line masking tape (#215),
Coast Automask, plastic wrap, chalk

I first started striping in 1996, more out of necessity than desire. I've been an airbrush professional since 1985, and I always let our local striping pro, Ron Beam, handle all the striping fun at the shop. Then one day, due to an emergency, Ron had to take off in the middle of a job. He never made it back to finish striping the graphics on this truck, so I had to finish the last color. Well, heck, I'm an airbrusher, I thought. I had lettered things, but never even held a striping brush. To be blunt, the result was nasty. So thinking quickly, I decided to turn the "elephant man" stripe into a slash effect. Using the same sword striper, I created a random overlapping "slashing" of lines to create a nice chaotic look. Besides hiding my nasty attempt at striping, the overall effect was a nice juxta-position to the rest of Ron's perfectly straight line work. The slash stripe technique was born! The funny thing is, I have gotten pretty good at striping, but my most requested style is still the slash. Go figure!

The slash striping accident is a typical kustom paint story—many great effects or techniques began life as accidents. Deadline pressure often forces artists to repair or change direction in a design when a mistake is made. These mishaps become the foundation for countless kustom tricks and techniques. I've even heard a story that the original decorative swirly-Q stripes that Dutch pioneered were first used to hide some grinder marks that were showing through the paint on the hood of a car.

As for striping, I've always appreciated the artistic design work of the hot rod industry. My favorites are the edgy pinstripe designs that have been labeled "Von Dutching." Whether it's the artwork of Jimmy C, Von Dutch, Ed Roth, Bob Spena, Bob Bond, Von Franco, or any other striping guru, these freeform designs are the heart of the kustom kulture. For this reason, I had to incorporate this style into my piece. I also wanted to include a character into the striping, much like Dutch's Harvey Shaken or Franco's Space Pussy. The minimalist design of the striping makes it very challenging to include characters while still maintaining a flowing line and symmetrical style. Of course, I had to throw in a lit-tle slash striping, just for mistakes!

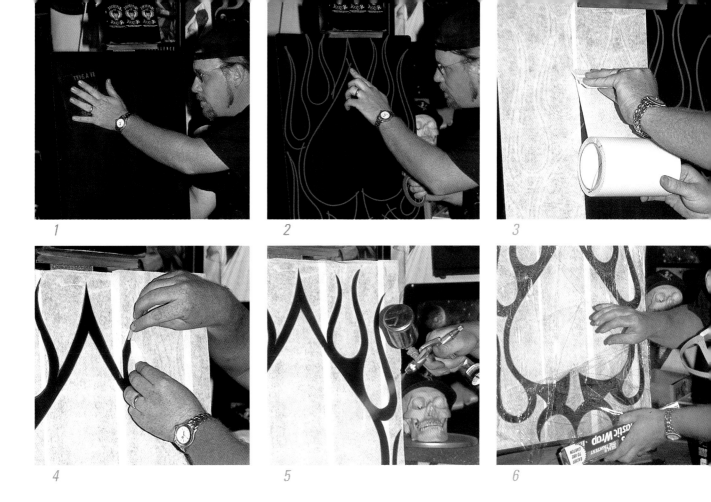

1   2   3

4   5   6

Step 1

I scuff the surface of a powder-coated aluminum sign blank with a red Scotch-Brite pad. This gives the surface a good tooth for the striping paint (and later clearcoat) to stick to. If I weren't going to apply clearcoat, I would just stripe right over the surface. After the surface is scuffed, I wipe the dust off using a little precleaner, to prepare the surface for the paint.

Step 2

To start my piece, I mask off and spray a graphic that I can then pinstripe (plus, I can't help using a little spraying and airbrushing in the design). Using some 3M Fine Line masking tape, I lay out a spade inner design, with the outside edge turning into flames. Must keep that hot rod retro theme going!

Step 3

To mask off my tape layout, I grab some Coast Automask. This product not only cuts more easily than masking tape, but it is also more transparent, so you can see the underlying design. Best of all, it's cheaper for masking large areas. When laying the masking down, you will need a vinyl application squeegee to get all the air bubbles out. I prefer the small roll to the larger one, as you end up with fewer wrinkles when applying it.

Step 4

With a standard razor blade, I cut out the design using the underlying blue tape as a guide. The tape also acts as a buffer to keep the blade from cutting into the base. Be sure to use a sharp blade when cutting tape. A dull blade is more likely to damage and score the underlying surface.

Step 5

Instead of paint, I use a little House of Kolor MB-01 silver/white marblizer. Using my Iwata RG-3, I spray an even wet coat of marblizer over the exposed surface. With a little stirring, the marblizer is ready to spray right from the can; there's no need for reducer. Marblizer works best over a dark surface. If you use it on any shade lighter than black, you can barely notice the pearlescent effect.

Step 6

While the marblizer is still wet, I apply some plastic wrap. Any type of material can be used for this "ragging" effect, but I prefer the thinness of the plastic wrap; it creates more wrinkles. The way the plastic is applied and removed has a significant effect on the finished product.

Craig Fraser

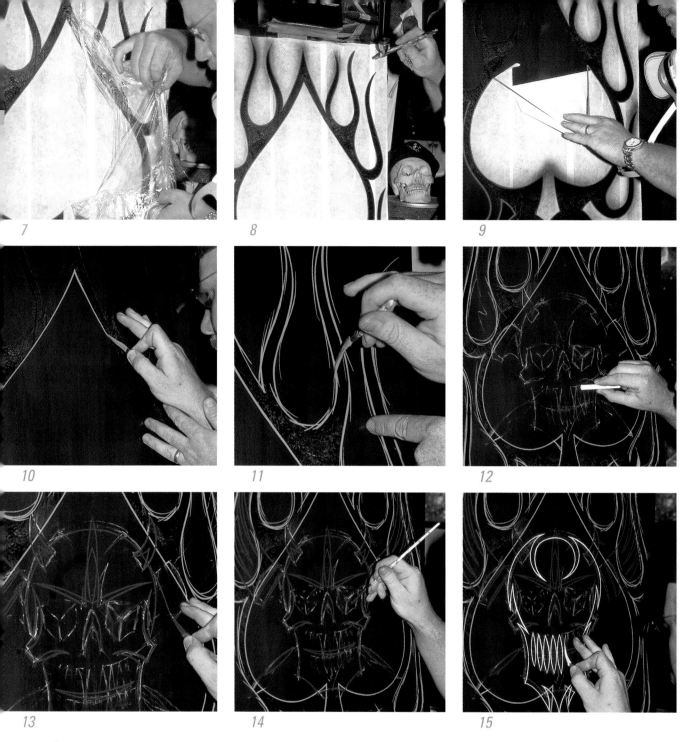

7

8

9

10

11

12

13

14

15

Step 7

I like to leave the wrap on until the marblizer sets. Then, when it's removed, it rips a little of the marblizer off, giving the design an interesting look. If you remove the plastic when the marblizer is still wet, lift it with care to avoid damaging your masterpiece.

Step 8

After letting the marblizer dry completely, I use my Iwata Eclipse CS to fade in some House of Kolor Purple Kandy. I add the Kandy Koncentrate to SG-100 to create a basecoat Kandy. The Kandy gives the marblizer a violet color, but allows all the pearl effect to shine through.

Step 9

Although it's pretty difficult to see until it's cleared, the violet marblizer snaps against the black background after it's unmasked. Just remember, marblizer is pretty weak. You can easily remove it with precleaner or lift it with tape. So when unmasking, be sure to remove the tape away from the painted surface so that it will not lift any edges.

Step 10

I mix up some lime green by combining House of Kolor Lemon Yellow and Green striping urethane, and then I begin striping the marblized design. For graphics and curving designs, I prefer the Xcaliber sword striper. The brush I'm using is a size #00.

16   17   18

Step 11

For the outside of the design, I keep the same color, but I switch to the infamous slash striping. Using this random slash pattern, I finish up the outline of the flame graphic.

Step 12

Using a piece of classroom chalk, I sketch out the basic design that I follow with the pinstriping. This sketch helps establish balance and keeps the design centered. I don't like using a Stabilo or waxed-based pencils, as they have a tendency to leave marks behind, especially when clearcoating.

Step 13

After cleaning my brush and switching to House of Kolor Roman Red striping urethane, I begin striping the centerpiece design. Because I am right-handed, I start on the left side of the design. This prevents my hand from resting in wet paint or blocking my line of sight.

Step 14

For the dots on the dice, I switch from my sword striper to a lettering quill. This allows me to brush in small details that would be difficult to do with a striping brush. I probably could have used this brush for the entire center design, but I prefer the tapered end lines of the striper.

Step 15

Switching back to my Xcaliber, I use House of Kolor White to punch out the skull design and render the teeth. It is very important to completely clean the brush when switching colors, especially with red. One molecule of red can turn a gallon of white to pink!

Step 16

I switch back to the liner brush to touch up any ends and to add a few finishing touches to the white, like my trademark #13 on the tooth.

Step 17

Using the same House of Kolor Lemon Yellow that I mixed to make the lime green earlier, I lay in the last color of my design. The yellow defines the crossed brushes in the background, as well as my skull's goatee and flame hairdo. I could probably add a few more colors, but I like to keep my decorative pinstriping simple.

Step 18

Don't forget the signature. Not signing your artwork is a cardinal sin in pinstriping, especially if you want to get credit for it later on.

Well, that's it. The only thing left is to clearcoat with House of Kolor UFC-19 urethane clear.

I may be a little unorthodox in my techniques, but I've always believed that in art, the end justifies the means. The best thing about kustom painting is the individuality of it. Kustom, by definition, has always gone against the grain, thumbing its nose at convention and the established way of doing things. Kustom painting is the art of the individual, and the painter must be an individual as well. This is true even if that individual is an airbrusher who just happened to get his hands on a pinstripe brush one day!

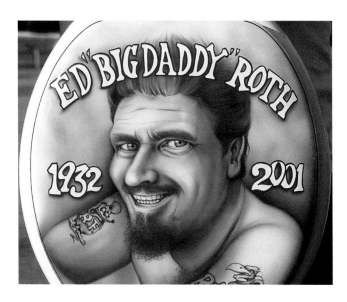

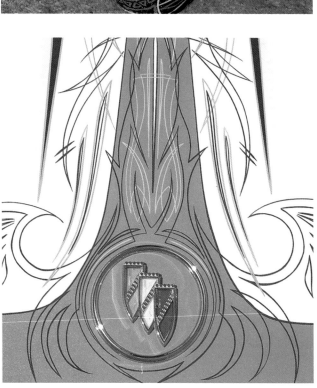

84

Craig Fraser

Screamin' Eagle
Jack "The Italian" Giachino

SUPPLIES

PAINT MEDIA: PPG mixing colors, House of Kolor urethane striping paint

BRUSHES: #2 script brush, #00 Mack striping brush, Paasche VL airbrush

OTHER: Frisket masking film, X-Acto knife, Stabilo pencil, 2,000-grit wet/dry sandpaper

Jack "The Italian" Giachino has been doing custom paint work and teaching art for more than 30 years. Raised on Von Dutch, Dean Jeffries, and Larry Watson, Giachino says he was "bit by the custom bug" at a very young age. Today he enjoys working with the mixed bag of multimedia techniques and styles he's picked up over the years. His shop, Giachino's Studios in Green Bay, Wisconsin, specializes in airbrush art, pinstriping, lettering, and design work.

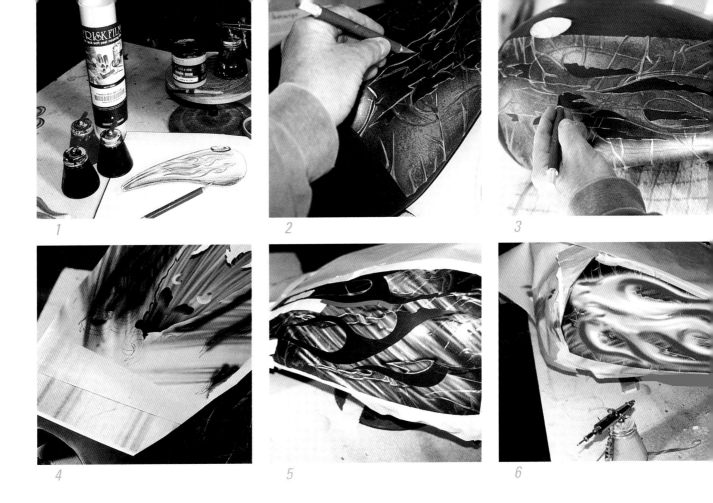

1   2   3

4   5   6

The success of any custom paint job depends on having two things: the proper tools and a plan. For this job, you'll need frisket masking film, an X-Acto knife, an airbrush, a pinstriping brush, and paint.

Step 1

Once I have all my materials, I sketch the flame layout and the eagle image to lay a strong foundation for my design.

Step 2

Next, I apply frisket film, a low-tack masking material, to both sides of the tank. I draw the flame and rip design directly onto the film with a white Stabilo pencil. Then I use my X-Acto knife to carefully cut the design.

Step 3

Care must be taken not to cut too deeply. Cuts that go well into the painted surface can cause serious problems down the road. I remove the ripped areas around the flames. This is the first part I'll airbrush.

Step 4

I tape a hand-cut stencil of the eagle's head and claw rips to the top of the tank. Using a combination of white, yellow, and red oxide, I airbrush random streaks from the top of the tank, angling forward to the sides. This color combination depicts the wrap of the eagle's wings.

Step 5

After I apply the rip in a random striated pattern, I replace the frisket film in these areas. The next step is to remove the frisket from both sides of the tank to reveal the flame pattern.

Step 6

I airbrush the yellow flame base color first, then follow this with a red under-shadow and a white highlight. The tank is sitting on a revolving pottery stand, which allows me to work from one side to the other with ease.

Jack Giachino

7

8

9

10

11

Step 7

After I remove the frisket film from both sides of the tank, the design starts to take shape. The paints I have used so far have all been PPG mixing colors (toners) that I have thinned to the proper consistency for airbrushing (approximately twice the recommended spray gun reduction).

Step 8

Using a photocopy machine, I make three copies of my original eagle design on card stock. This allows me to cut out different parts for different colors. More importantly, it allows for perfect register of all the elements, since all three are exact copies.

Step 9

I mask the stencils to define the sharp edges in the design. Next, I freehand the soft-edge areas with a Paasche VL airbrush, my model of choice for the past 30 years.

Step 10

With the bulk of the airbrushing complete, it's time for the finishing touches. I use a #2 script brush to add details and highlights. Note, the micro-signature. You have to advertise whenever you can!

Step 11

The flames wouldn't be complete without pinstriping. I'm using a #00 brush and House of Kolor urethane striping paint. The urethane paint ensures that I can clear over this project without any fear of the pinstriping lifting.

Step 12

The finished pinstriping adds a framing effect to the flames. Just as the frame completes a picture, the pinstriping completes the flames.

I have cleared the tank, color-sanded it with 2,000-grit wet/dry sandpaper, buffed it, and reassembled it. There's nothing left to do but get the motor running and go screaming down the highway!

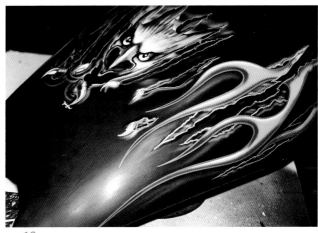

12

Jack Giachino

Laying Down the Line
Harry Henkel

SUPPLIES

PAINT MEDIA: 1-Shot® Lettering Enamel
BRUSHES: Xcaliber striping brushes, outliner brush
or lettering quill
OTHER: Wax and grease remover

No matter how well your striping job turns out, it's worthless if it doesn't last. The most important first step in a good striping job is to remove any dirt, grease, and wax from the painting surface. I usually like to wash the surface with water and alcohol first, then go back over it with a high-quality wax and grease remover to make sure the surface is squeaky clean.

Most sign painters and pinstripers use 1-Shot lettering enamel, which is made to cover with one

coat and hold up against the elements. Brushes are a matter of personal preference. My favorite is the Xcaliber, which is available from Mr. J at Xcaliber Corporation in Lyndhurst, New Jersey. These brushes are shorter than regular striping brushes and allow for greater control. Another excellent maker of brushes is Mack. Experiment with different brands until you find what works for you. In addition to a striping brush, an outliner brush or lettering quill can come in handy for tight curves.

You can lightly sketch your design right onto the surface you are striping using a water-based Stabilo pencil or china marker. Another layout method is to use a pounce pattern, which is a design drawn on a piece of paper and then perforated using a pounce wheel or

electro-pounce machine. You place the pattern on the vehicle and rub chalk on it. When you fold the paper in half, your design will be symmetrical. I've got countless patterns with my favorite striping designs on them. Here are some basic designs.

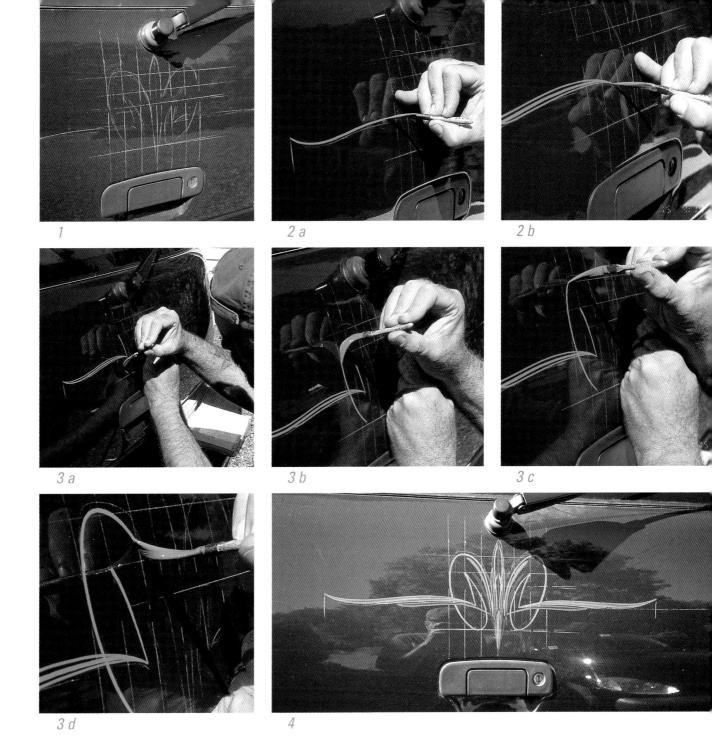

1

2 a

2 b

3 a

3 b

3 c

3 d

4

Step 1

After surface prep, I use the grid method to ensure that both sides are mirrored. I palette my brush on a magazine, and sparingly add thinner to achieve the desired paint consistency. It requires a little experience to know exactly how you want the paint to feel. Try to have just enough paint in the brush to ensure that all the brush hair is wet. Too much paint in the brush will produce runs, drips, or lines that are too thick. For pinstriping, I prefer colors that are subtle and don't contrast with the background.

Step 2

Hold the brush at a 90-degree angle using just the very tip for striping. Use your pinky as a guide to keep your hand at an even distance from the surface. This should produce a long thick flowing line. Being right-handed, I like to start from the left and work to the right.

Step 3

For curly lines, I hold the brush like this, twirling it between my fingers. If you do not twirl the brush as you turn it, the line's thickness will not be consistent.

Step 4

After the basic design has dried, I usually add a second or third color of even less contrast. This adds to the design without competing with the original colors.

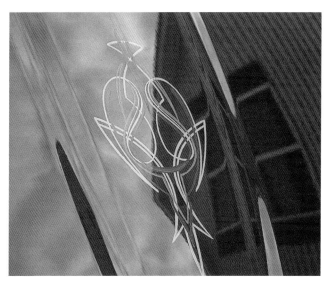
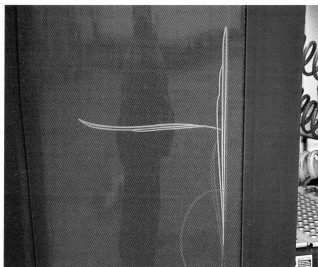

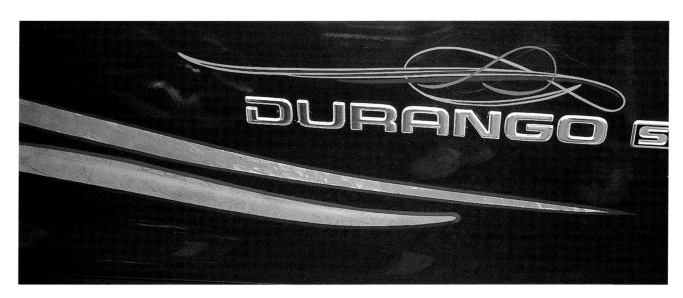

Master of the Fine Line

Hot Rod

SUPPLIES

PAINT MEDIA: 1-Shot® Lettering Enamel
BRUSHES: #00 Xcaliber striping brush

Well, stripers and striperettes, it's Hot Rod here.
Today's lesson is how to do the fine line. No, it's not the latest line dance or a new slang term—the fine line is simply pinstriping at its best. For those kats and kittens who know me, hold on; this is the slow part. For the rest of you, here's the skinny: My name is Hot Rod and I'm a pinstriper. You may know me as the founder of Hot Rod's, the store I ran in Norco, California. Before I sold it in 2001, the store featured "kustom kulture" art, car parts, accessories, movies, posters, and more. We would even host striping bashes and live music. Most of the lines I lay are considered an art form. Though I do kustom cars, I'm also known for the small stuff, like cell phones, Hotwheels cars, models, girls' purses...I guess what I'm trying to say is that I do all kinds of stuff, even things you wouldn't normally think to pinstripe.

I want to cover a few things before we get started. Normally, my lines are very thin and hard to photograph. So in order for you to see them, I had to fatten them up a bit. As for equipment, I use a #00 Xcaliber brush, uncut, and 1-Shot paint. One last thing: If you know anything about striping, forget it. I break all the rules.

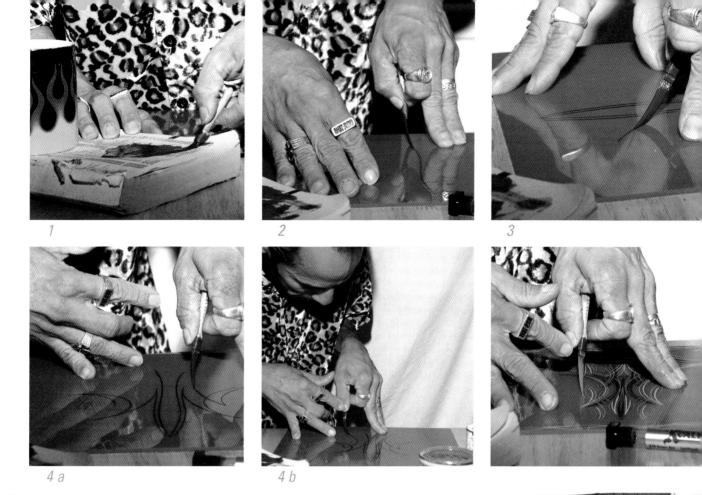

1 2 3

4 a 4 b

Step 1

I load my brush with 1-Shot paint, straight out of the can. When you use the paint straight out of the can, it's easier to lay down a thin line without the paint running or bleeding. I use a phone book to palette my brush. The phone book has a big drag—it will pull more paint out of the brush than other paletting surfaces will. Once you have the paint on your palette, drop your brush in the paint and drag it left and right. It may take some time to get a feel for how much paint to leave on the brush. When "thin-lining," you only need a very small amount.

Step 2

Now I lay the line. As you can see in the photo, I'm only using the tip of the brush, and my two inner fingers are fully extended to act as a guide. In this stance, it's hard to stay consistent, so start slowly. If you increase or decrease the pressure on your hand, you'll change the thickness of the line.

Step 3

I always stripe with only about one-quarter of the tip of the brush, even when laying lines on the trunk of a lead sled! Depending on the piece, I can lay only about three or four lines before I have to reload my brush.

Step 4

You can see that even when I do turns, I still use just the tip of the brush. When I turn, I use both

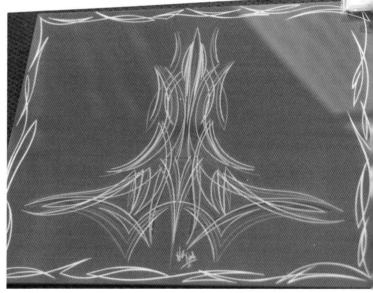

hands to guide me. By doing this, your line stays mirrored from left to right. The key to thin is pressure! By the way, the photos aren't backward. I'm left-handed. (Cool shirt, huh?)

We're finished with our piece! With time, practice, and a whole lot of patience, you can master the fine line!

Pinstriping, Japanese Style
Takahiro "Wildman" Ishii

SUPPLIES

PAINT MEDIA: 1-Shot® Lettering Enamel
BRUSHES: Mack striping brushes
OTHER: Dermatograph China marker

In this how-to, Japanese pinstriper Takahiro "Wildman" Ishii brings his signature automotive art to a pair of leather pants for an incredible hot rod look. When asked what he thought was the standard that pinstripers should be judged by—speed, style, or accuracy—he said that all of those are important, but in his eyes, consistency in line stroke weight is a true measure of a striper's skill. No matter what level striper you are though, Ishii stresses practice, practice, and more practice! Follow along with him for a chance to hone those striping skills with this very wearable example of kustom kulture.

1

2

3 a

3 b

4

5

6

7

Step 1
Hiro starts by sketching a rough draft using a Dermatograph China marker.

Step 2
He then draws the flames by hand using 1-Shot enamel.

Step 3
Using an airbrush, Hiro draws the familiar Mack brush onto the pants and begins his flamed out background.

Step 4
Next, he pinstripes his idea onto the leather pants.

Step 5
Hiro draws a '57 Ford on one pant leg using the airbrush and pinstripe brush.

Step 6
Hiro stripes a spider web using his brush.

Step 7
Here's the finished backside of the pants.

Takahiro "Wildman" Ishii

This project took approximately two days to complete, back and front, as one side had to dry before the other side could be painted. It was auctioned off at Mooneyes Hot Rod Custom Show in Japan.

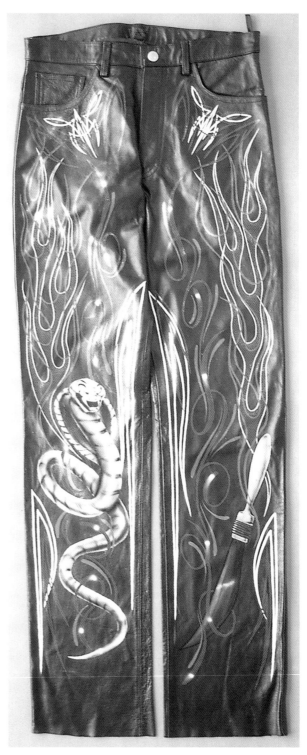

Alan Johnson

SUPPLIES

PAINT MEDIA: 1-Shot® Lettering Enamel
BRUSHES: Mack striping brushes
OTHER: 3M™ Finesse tape;
    1-Shot® Fast Dry Gold Size (#4008),
    High Temp Reducer (#6002),
    Super Gloss Tinting Clear (#4006)

Recently I got a request from Hibernia Auto Restoration in Hibernia, New Jersey, to add the finishing touches to a 1931 Packard Dietrich. More than 70 years ago, custom body builder Raymond Dietrich built this car. It was one of three cars Dietrich displayed at the Custom Salon auto show in Chicago in 1930, where King Gustav V of Sweden bought it. The car found its way back to the United States in 1951, but it was never fully restored until 2000. Follow along as I put the gold leaf striping on this classic.

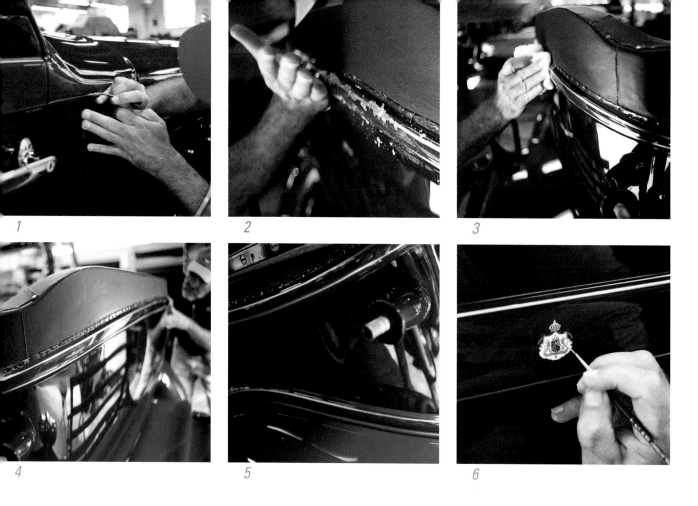

1

2

3

4

5

6

Step 1

After I clean the surface with wax and grease remover, I mix 1-Shot Fast Dry Gold Size with a few drops of white for maximum stripe coverage and consistency. The brush I use for this is the Equalizer. Created by Jim Farr, my friend and fellow striper, this brush runs a very fine line.

Step 2

The gold size takes about an hour to set up, depending on weather conditions. I carefully apply 23-karat patent gold to the stripe. Then I gently tap the gold with the heel of my hand. This ensures complete coverage as the loose gold is picked up and carried to any missed areas.

Step 3

Using cotton, I lightly burnish the gold, following the body lines in one direction. This flattens the gold and gives it an even brilliance as the light reflects. I follow with a coat of 1-Shot Super Gloss Tinting Clear and a few drops of hardener with the same brush.

Step 4

When I come back the next morning, the clear is dry. I clean the surface vigorously with damp cotton and a touch of Bon Ami to remove any gold that has adhered to surface. With a mixture of Maroon and Bright Red 1-Shot and a few drops of turpentine, I start striping with the same brush again.

Step 5

Striping around the edge of any color is difficult and takes a lot of practice. As with everything in life, it's a question of balance. You must keep the space between the gold and red lines consistent. I've found that it helps to step back occasionally to make sure all your lines are even. You can quickly remove any mistakes with 1-Shot High Temp Reducer.

Step 6

The owner of Hibernia Auto Restoration is an expert on Packard automobiles. His research was most helpful in supplying me with a color copy of *Greater Coat Of Arms*. I painted this with #2/0 and #4/0 Alan Johnson Signature brushes by Mack.

It's always a good feeling to step back and see the finished product—even better when your work takes first place at the Pebble Beach Concourse! After more than 30 years of striping and lettering, there's still nothing like working on a classic.

Alan Johnson

Freehand Originals
Steve Kafka

SUPPLIES

PAINT MEDIA: 1-Shot® Lettering Enamel
BRUSHES: #3 and #6 Dick Blick 4901 brushes

As a pinstriper, developing a feel for composition is a combination of natural and learned abilities. The inspiration for me is the gratification, both verbal and monetary, and the beauty of this flowing art form, considered by many to be the only true "American" art form.

My designs are totally spontaneous. The Kafka style is a never-ending metamorphosis of design, flow, and color that has changed thousands of times in the past 30 years. I look forward to seeing what develops in the future. Designs like the one pictured here usually take less than ten minutes to complete and no two are alike. Two galleries currently sell these matted paper panels for $250 each.

This panel is a horizontal centerpiece design. To complete it, I use Dick Blick 4901 brushes in sizes #3 and #6, trimmed at the ferrel, and 1-Shot enamel in Emerald Green, Process Blue, magenta, white, and orange.

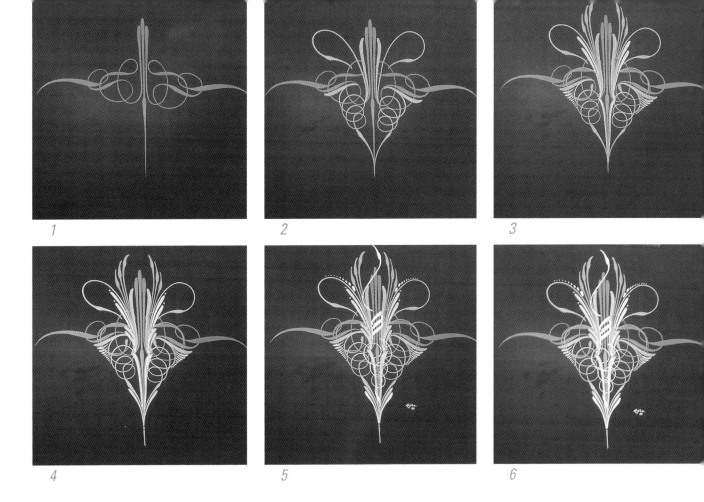

Step 1
I do my center line first, followed by the left-side design and then the right-side design.

Step 2
I lighten my first color for weight in the composition.

Step 3
I lighten again for fade and composition.

Step 4
I introduce the fourth color from the same family.

Step 5
Now I lighten the fourth color for continuation of fade and design.

Step 6
I lighten the color again for a three-color fade design extension.

Sign and deliver! It's all done.

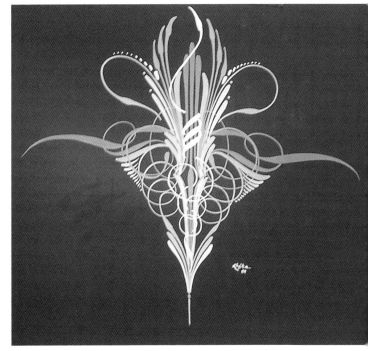

Steve Kafka

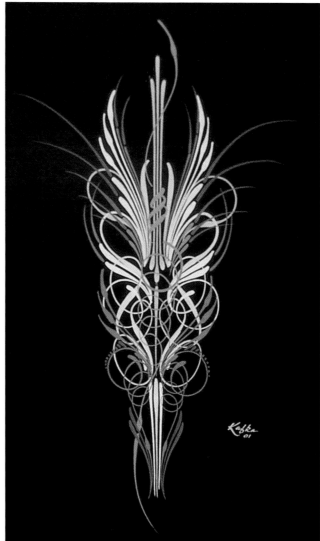

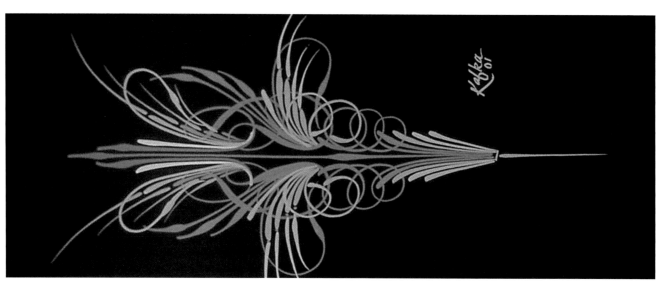

Steve Kafka

Pinstriping a Motorcycle Tank
Jon Kosmoski

SUPPLIES

PAINT MEDIA: House of Kolor striping paint
BRUSHES: #00 striping brushes
OTHER: 600-grit sandpaper

The founder of House of Kolor, Jon Kosmoski began painting friends' helmets and motorcycle parts shortly after high school. By the mid '60s, he was manufacturing his own line of kustom finishes while operating a body shop specializing in quality crash work. In 1983, after winning more than a hundred "Best Paint" awards at car shows nationwide, Jon closed the body shop to keep up with the growing demand for his paint products. That same year, he introduced his Kosmic Urethane kustom paints, and his business grew explosively. By the mid '90s, House of Kolor's sales were in the millions. Jon sold the company to the Valspar Corporation, where he remains an active consultant working on new products.

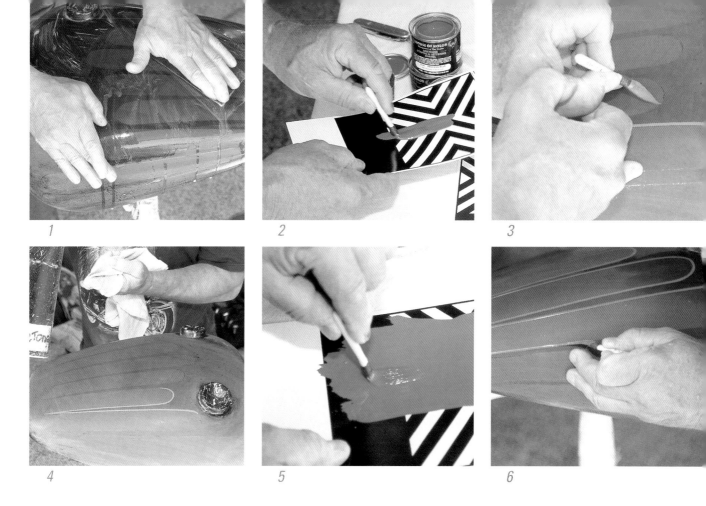

1

2

3

4

5

6

This project uses House of Kolor's pure acrylic urethane pinstriping paint. You can use these paints without a catalyst if you're going to clearcoat them. If not, use KU-200 catalyst. Because these paints are low build with high pigmentation, they're easy to level with clearcoats, and they are excellent for airbrush use with reduction.

Our pinstripe paints are available in a wide range of colors, including pastels. Pinstriping brushes come in various sizes, from #5 (the biggest) to #0000, the smallest. For this project, I use #00 brushes.

Step 1

It's important to apply the pinstriping to a catalyzed topcoat. This tank has already been cleared, but before pinstriping, we'll wet-sand it with 500- or 600-grit paper. Remember that when striping without KU-200 catalyst, wet-sanding the area ensures adhesion of both the pinstripe paint and the final clearcoats.

Step 2

Pulling the paint from a palette is very important—it gives you a chance to feel the paint before you begin the application. I put some of the Process Blue (U-30) on the card and then add U-00 reducer until the paint has the right consistency. I recommend paletting the paint on a hard surface. Some artists use phone books, but we don't

recommend that because the paper will absorb the solvents. You'll need a hard glossy surface that won't absorb the solvents, but will allow you to work the paint into the hair of the brush.

Step 3

I always support one hand with the other while striping. Pulling a straight line means first working enough paint up into the heel of the brush so that you don't run out halfway down the line. Always be sure the brush remains flexible. If it's not, return to the palette and add U-00 to make sure the brush is loose.

Step 4

Our urethane striping enamel is easy to use—any mistakes can be easily wiped off with a little acetone on a rag.

Step 5

When you return to the card for more paint, you can feel the tension in the paint. Add more paint or reducer as needed to create just the right consistency. You must also work some paint up into the heel of the brush, a skill that comes with practice.

Step 6

To run a nice straight line, you need good technique and a paintbrush that carries enough paint to complete the line without having to stop and go back to the card.

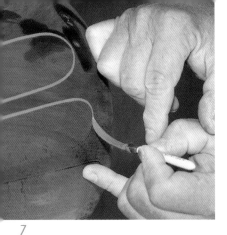

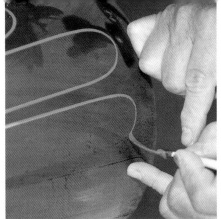

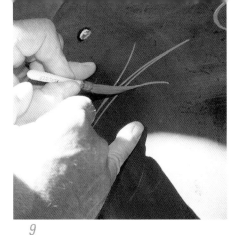

7

8

9

Step 7

Corners require that you lift and twist the brush or you'll get an inconsistent line. For tight turns, reload the brush to ensure adequate paint flow.

Step 8

Here, I rotate the brush as I stripe the curve. If you don't rotate the brush, it will flatten out and the line will vary in width as you go around the circle.

Step 9

At the front of the tank, I add some freehand striping in an abstract pattern. Before finishing, I use a second color, Hot Pink U-27, to add another dimension to the pinstripe design.

A: The finished tank before clearcoating.

B: The tank after clearcoating. I sanded between clearcoats to produce a perfectly smooth surface.

C: This illustrates what happens when clear is applied too heavily. Note the way the pinstripes have run. This is also caused by an inadequate wait between coats. Always make sure the paint is dry before you apply the next coat. If your clearcoater likes to use heavy coats, you may want to consider adding more catalyst to the striping paint to help alleviate color-pulling.

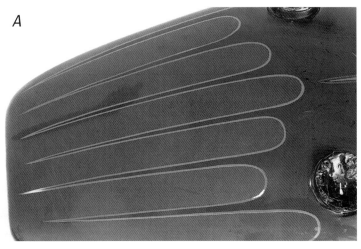

A

B

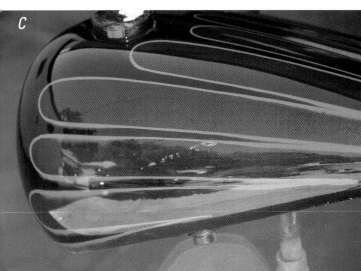

C

Mike Lavallee

SUPPLIES

PAINT MEDIA: 1-Shot® Lettering Enamel
BRUSHES: Mike Lavallee pictorial brushes,
American Painter #4050 script brush
OTHER: Saral paper, wax and grease remover,
window cleaner

Pinstriping and murals come in a huge variety of styles, from the traditional striping of the '50s to the scroll and high-tech artwork of today. When I started painting in 1979, I struggled to find a style that was purely my own. I went through many changes, mostly by studying other artists' work. By borrowing a piece here and there and combining it with my own style, I was able to come up with something new.

One thing I did was to combine my love for painting wildlife with my own style of pinstriping to create something I call "pic-striping," which merges pictures and stripes. The new look was an immediate hit with my clients. This article will take you through one of my projects. My technique for hand-painted pictorial work is a dry-brush method, where I build up colors by loosely applying one color over the next with very little thinner used in the paint. Of course, this is not the only way to paint, but it works for me. Give pic-striping a try. It's a lot of fun, and you'll open a whole new world for yourself!

Remember this phrase: dark to light, loose to tight. Whenever I start a piece, I always work from my darkest colors to my lightest. I keep things super loose and gradually get tighter and brighter with my details and colors until I reach my goal. You may find this method confusing at first, but when you see your artwork develop, you'll understand why this works so well. Painting this way allows you to work faster and produces pictures with more life.

The first thing I recommend is to find excellent reference material. Nothing can replace a great photo of your subject. This will help you get started and serve as your guide to detail and color. Also, when choosing a picture, select one that works well with the shape of the panel you'll paint on. For instance, an eagle head profile works better on the side of a motorcycle tank than it would, say, on the top of the tank.

For this project, I use different types of brushes than most of you are accustomed to. For the mural part, I use the Mike Lavallee pictorial brushes manufactured by Mack. These brushes are a blend of solvent-proof synthetic fibers that are designed to take a beating when it comes to pictorial work.

For the pinstriping part, I prefer an American Painter #4050 script brush in a size 4, available at Michael's craft stores. This extremely versatile brush does amazing things, all for less than five dollars!

Another handy item is Saral paper, a graphite paper that comes in different colors. For this project, I use white Saral paper. I find white to be the most useful of all the colors—you can paint right over it without the fish-eye that can occur when using regular carbon paper. All the paint I use is 1-Shot lettering enamels.

First, I always clean the surface of whatever I'm working on with a good wax and grease remover. Then I wipe the surface with window cleaner to remove any residue from the wax and grease remover. After cleaning, I usually give the surface the old finger squeak test to ensure that it's completely free of wax.

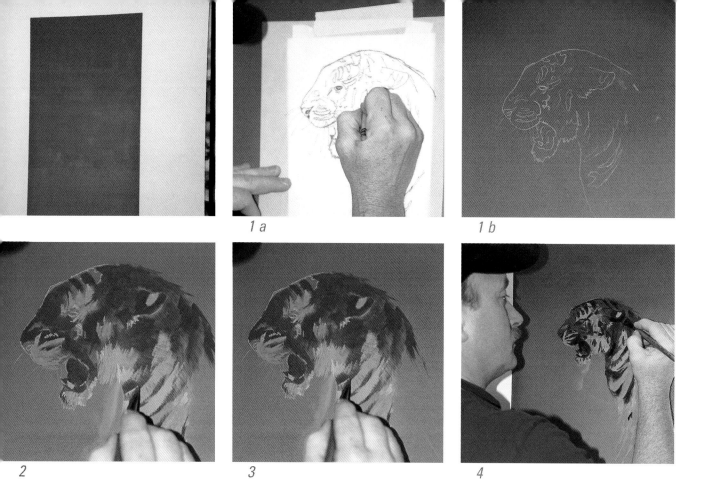

1 a

1 b

2

3

4

Step 1

I tape the sketch of my tiger to the panel and place the white Saral paper under the sketch. Note: Make sure the chalky side is down before you start to trace your picture. Only the chalky side will leave a traced image for you to follow. I trace over the major shapes of the tiger. You don't have to trace all the little details—I go over the outer body shape, eye, nose, mouth, white patches, and black stripes. Now you can see the tiger transferred on the panel.

Step 2

I start painting! I use very little thinner. I want my paint to drag slightly and break up when I apply it. This is called a dry-brush effect. By doing this, I allow each color to be seen though the next so that each layer works together to create a whole piece. I'll use the 1/2-inch flat Lavallee brush for the bulk of this pictorial. When I load the brush, I'll palette off about 50% of the paint to avoid flooding the color.

I start with orange mixed about 50-50 with Proper Purple to get a brownish purple color. If the paint becomes too "sticky," I dip slightly into a thinner cup. I dry-brush the dark color where the orange of the tiger is. I paint in the direction of the hair,

constantly referring to my original photo for the correct look. My strokes are shorter where the hair is shorter and longer where it is longer. Don't be too concerned with making this first step perfect. Remember, loose to tight! I lay in some loose detail to show the nose outline and the teeth.

Step 3

Next, I mix a bit of white, black, and purple to get the dark color for the base of all the white. I paint this the same way I did the first color, letting the paint break apart as I go along. Some of the original panel color should still be visible through the paint at this point. Note: I'm slightly overlapping the purple and white paint over my first color.

Step 4

Now I move on to roughing in the black stripes and dark colors in the mouth area. For this step, I'm going to mix purple and orange with a touch of black to make a brownish color. This is the only step where I don't go dark to light. I roughly paint in the brown color with the same "hair" strokes in all the areas I traced out for the tiger's stripes and then, more solidly, in the mouth area. To soften the stripes and make them look more realistic, I use brown

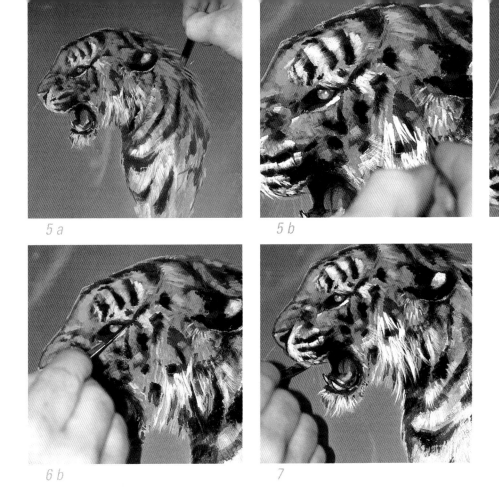

5 a

5 b

6 a

6 b

7

first, instead of going right to black. Otherwise, the stripes would just be stark black. When I do add black, I blend the color only within the brown I already painted, leaving some of that brown color showing around the edges.

Step 5

Now I'm going to bring the cat to life! Take straight orange and palette some into your brush. Remember to take most of it out by paletting on a magazine page so only a medium amount of paint remains on the hairs. Next, I start the whole process over by brushing the hair over the darker color I painted first. I also let the first color show through a bit to add depth to the hair. You can lighten this color some more by adding a touch of white or yellow, in smaller amounts where you see brighter highlights in your original reference photo. I also add some of the orange color to the eye and highlight it with the lighter yellow-orange color.

I do the same thing to the areas that I'll paint white, repeating the same process I use for the orange, only this time I use straight white. While I have the white out, I mix up a little pinkish brown and paint the nose and tongue. Then I lighten up that color and highlight these areas.

Step 6

It's time to use the black paint. As I mentioned earlier, when I paint in the black on the stripes, I paint only the centers with the "hair" strokes and leave a bit of the original color showing around the edges. It's like a "glow line," if you will!

Next, I move on to the mouth. At this point, switch to the script brush to do some of the smaller line details, such as outlining the teeth and detailing around the eye and nose.

Step 7

It's time to finesse the cat's coat with all the little details in the white fur. To do this, I'll usually look for spots that need to be punched up. I might add some flare to the fur around the cheek area, and then go in and add some small white highlights to the nose and eye.

Mike Lavallee

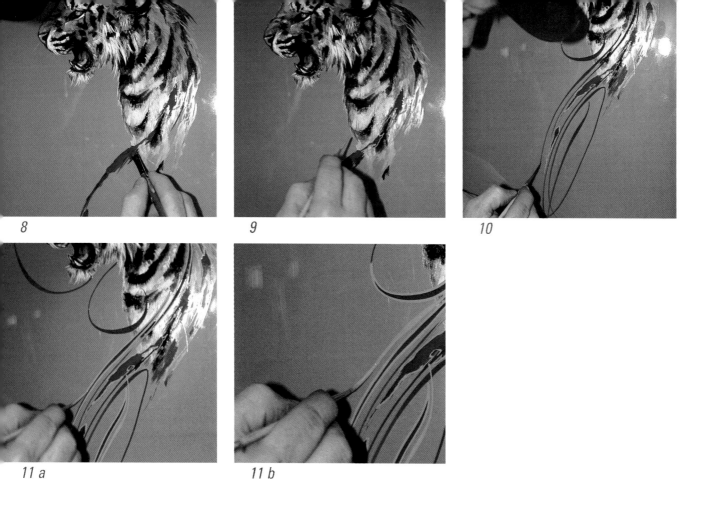

8

9

10

11 a

11 b

Step 8

The cat is almost complete. We just have to jazz this picture up with some color! Some of the coolest color combinations are found in nature.

If you want to blow your mind with color combinations, check out books on insects, seashells, tropical fish, and flowers! You won't believe some of the combinations you'll discover.

I love putting hot colors against cool ones. For this picture I start by using Reflex Blue and dry-brushing some graphic shreds. I load the brush as before, taking most of the paint off. Then, using the corner of the 1/2-inch Lavallee pictorial brush, I start at the top of the tiger's head and paint small ragged strokes in a broken fashion. The strokes get larger the further away from the head I work, in the same way that the hairs are smaller at the front of the head, growing gradually longer as they go back.

I'll usually swing this pattern across and in front of my picture. I'll also add touches of blue to the black fur on the ears and the fleshy part of the mouth. I like adding little tiny specks of this color here and there to add "color tension" to the piece.

Step 9

To punch it up even more, I mix a "slime green" using 1-Shot Lemon Yellow, Kansas City Teal, and a touch of Process Blue. Then I take the script brush again and paint a broken outline around the blue shreds.

Step 10

The next step is to put some action lines around the cat with some scroll-type pinstriping. Using purple and the script brush, I paint some sweeping loops around the tiger's head and neck. My lines are thin to start, but as I loop around, I gradually press harder on the brush to achieve the thicker part of the stroke and then lighten up near the end of the stripe.

This part takes practice to develop the correct speed and movement. You'll notice I use the hand-over-hand method to hold my brush. I use both hands at the same time—they move as one. I use my left hand mainly as a brace on which to support and roll my right hand, and I use my right hand to maneuver the brush through the loops and sweeps of my strokes. Note: My left hand almost NEVER touches the surface while I paint. The only time it makes contact with the surface is when I start the stroke or when I need to brace my right hand while I'm painting the little details.

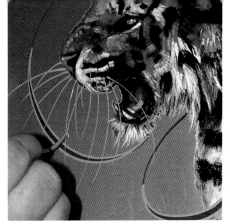

12 a

12 b

As you can see, I've looped a stroke around the tiger's head to frame it. I think it makes a nice touch.

Step 11

Next, I mix a yellow-orange color to outline the thicker strokes of my purple pinstripes. With the same yellow-orange, I build on what I've already painted with stripes similar to the purple stripes I painted first, but this time I don't outline them.

Step 12

I'm just about done with my pinstriping. My next and final step is to give the tiger his whiskers. I wait until the end to do this because I like to have the whiskers go over the pinstriping. It would be almost impossible to do it the other way around. I take orange and a touch of purple and paint in the whiskers. Then, as before, I lighten up the mixture and highlight the whiskers.

Well, there you have it—a complete pic-striped design. With some practice, you'll be creating all kinds of combinations and creations! This is a fun way to add some zip to a boring pictorial. Don't be afraid to experiment with different looks and color combinations. After all, it's just paint!

Speed King

Makoto

SUPPLIES

PAINT MEDIA: 1-Shot® Lettering Enamel
BRUSHES: Mack striping brushes
OTHER: Stabilo pencil

In the late 1990s, Japanese pinstripers began to make their way to the United States to attend local kustom kulture events and to bring their art to hot rod shows stateside. One of the Japanese shops to successfully enter the North American kustom market is M&K Custom Signs, owned and operated by 35-year-old Makoto Kobayashi.

After splashing onto the American scene, Makoto was named "Speed King" in the striping contest at the Rat Fink party in 2000. Since 1998, Makoto has also participated in many of the Rat Fink reunions at Mooneyes headquarters in Santa Fe Springs, California, as well as Jimmy C's and Dena Lux's Auto Art shows in Dana Point, California. These days, if there is a kustom hot rod or striping show, it's a safe bet Makoto will be there with his striping box in hand.

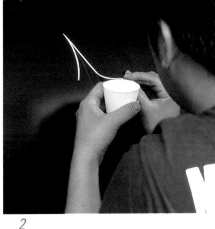

1

2

3

4

5

6

Step 1

Using a tape edge as guide, Makoto lays out his center line with a Stabilo pencil.

Step 2

Using 1-Shot White, Makoto begins with an arrowhead shape crowning the top of his design.

Step 3

Makoto connects his next set of lines with the main body of his design using a series of figure-eight shaped lines. Notice how he uses his pinky to anchor his brush strokes for maximum stability.

Step 4

For shorter lines like this one, Makoto uses just one hand as he paints.

Step 5

As the design grows, Makoto keeps his lines centered and both sides symmetrical, two of the most important ingredients in good pinstriping.

Step 6

Makoto moves on to the next set of lines.

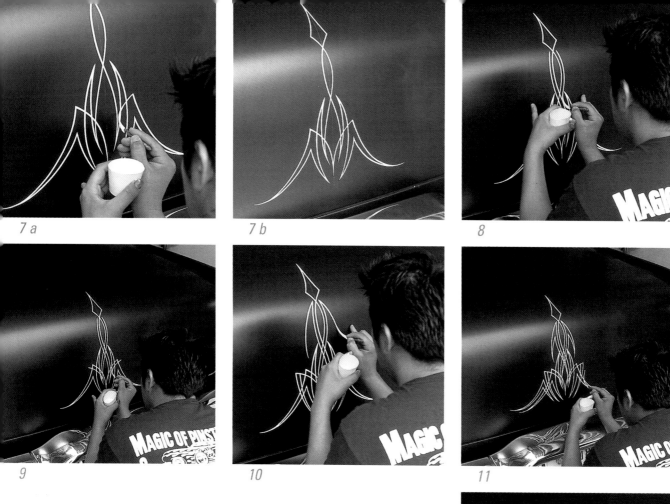

7 a

7 b

8

9

10

11

12

Step 7

At this point, Makoto completes the white portion of his design. Now he's ready to move on to his second color, yellow. Photo 7A shows the complete first half of the design.

Step 8

Next, Makoto adds yellow lines on both the inside and the outside of his original white lines.

Step 9

Makoto continues to use yellow lines to complete the white foundation of his design.

Step 10

With his eye on the reference line, Makoto keeps both sides of the design balanced.

Step 11

The design becomes more intricate as Makoto adds more complicated lines, always being careful to keep the line weight (thickness) consistent throughout all parts of the design.

Step 12

As Makoto nears the end of the job, he adds several curved lines to accent his overall design.

13

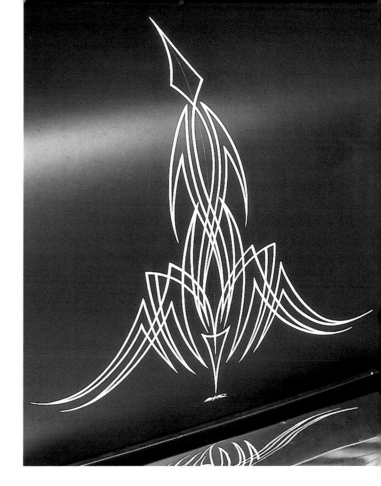

Step 13

Makoto adds a final line that runs alongside the curved line he painted in the previous step. He adds his signature, and he's done.

Makoto

The Line Doctor
Herb Martinez

SUPPLIES

PAINT MEDIA: 1-Shot® Lettering Enamel
BRUSHES: #00 Mack sword striper
OTHER: 1/4-inch 3M™ crepe tape, 3M™ white
masking paper (#6539), 3M™ Fine Line masking
tape (#215), Griffold #9 pounce wheel, chalk or
pounce bag, sea sponge

Herb Martinez has been involved with custom painting and pinstriping since he was 12 years old. Now, at age 57, his striping brush takes him around the world to shows in the United States, Europe, and Japan. Over the years, Herb has picked up pinstriping techniques from some of the top men in the business. Legendary Tommy "The Greek" was the first pro he ever saw stripe. Since then, Herb has found mentors in greats such as "Saint" John Morton, Red Lee, Steve Fineberg, Ken Tomashiro, and perhaps his greatest influence, Cary Greenwood, who hired Herb in 1978 for Classic Vans in Fremont, California. This job permanently changed the course of his professional career.

Herb is a man who definitely gives credit where credit is due. He has a long list of major influences but perhaps his most important laurel is that he is a past recipient of the Von Dutch pinstripe award from the Oakland Roadster show. Only a very exclusive club of stripers can lay claim to that. Watch as the "Line Doctor" shows off his incomparable striping skills in this demonstration.

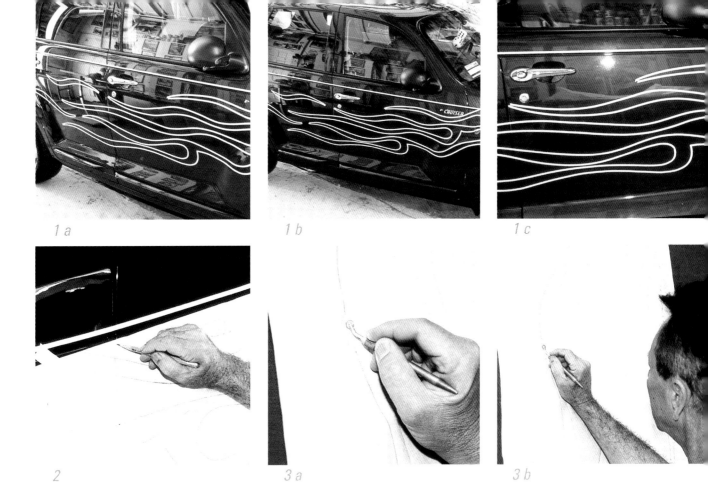

1 a   1 b   1 c

2   3 a   3 b

Step 1

On this PT Cruiser, my clients want two different styles of flames—the old classic style on the hood and a modern elongated style on the sides. I call this new style "snake" flames, a style popularized in the San Francisco Bay area back in the early '70s. I lay the side design using a freehand technique with 1/4-inch 3M crepe tape. The 1/4-inch tape turns a better curve than thicker tapes; it lays flat and gives a good surface to mask up to.

Step 2

After I lay out the flames on one side, I cover up the design with 3M white masking paper. This allows me to trace the design to match the other side. Using a #2 pencil, I trace the existing flames by running the pencil on the edge of the tape under the paper.

Step 3

With the tracing finished, I lay the paper on my layout board (you can use a table with a felt cover). I then take my Griffold #9 pounce wheel and start pouncing the pattern. This wheel punches small holes along the pencil line to help me transfer the design to the other side of the PT later.

Herb Martinez

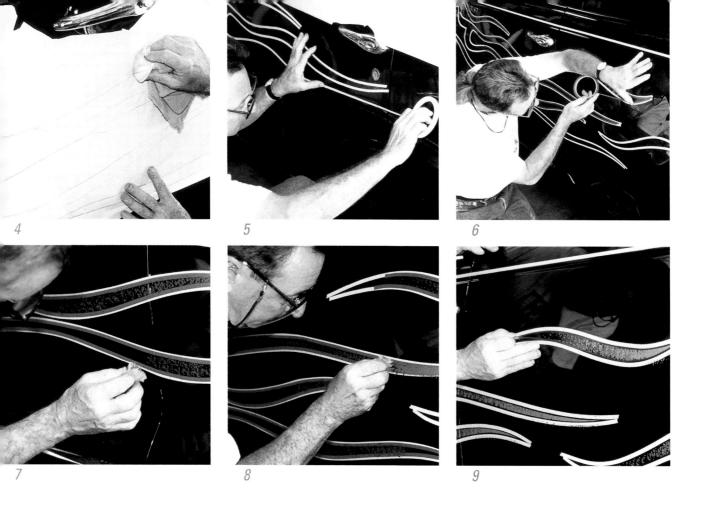

4

5

6

7

8

9

Step 4

I position the pounced paper on the opposite side of the PT. Using a chalk (or pounce) bag, pat the surface until all the holes in the pounced pattern have been chalked. Then carefully lift the paper to make sure the pounce transferred well enough to trace with your tape.

Step 5

A good rule of thumb: Don't completely remove the pattern right away. I lift mine above the design—that way if something happens to the chalk lines, I can always drop the pattern back into place. Using the same crepe tape, I trace the design left by the chalk. This gives me the exact design on both sides.

Step 6

After making sure the tape is laid out correctly, I use some compressed air and a tack rag to erase any leftover chalk dust. This is also a good time to pull off the pattern and wipe off any dust on the rest of the PT Cruiser that may hinder your painting.

Step 7

I lay in some 3M Fine Line masking tape (#215) about 1/8-inch inside the crepe tape. This gives me a natural border on the inside of the flame layout for

my sponge work. Using Magenta 1-Shot, I create a sponge effect with a piece of sea sponge, dabbing the paint in a gradated pattern, almost like an air-brushed fade, but coarser.

Step 8

After finishing with the Magenta, I go to the Purple and continue the sponging to create a two-color texture. Though I am using 1-Shot in this design, you can use House of Kolor instead, if you want a shorter dry time or if you plan to clearcoat later. I'm using 1-Shot on this job because the design on this PT Cruiser is going on top of the clear.

Step 9

With the sponging finished, I carefully remove the tape, leaving my 1/8-inch gap to stripe in. The masking and gap not only make the striping easier and faster, but since the pinstripe fills in the gap, I have less overall edge, allowing the flames to last longer. I lay out the pinstripe using Process Blue 1-Shot and a #00 Mack sword striper.

Step 10

Make sure to pull your tape before it completely dries—this allows the paint to fold over slightly, and give a more rounded line, without that nasty edge.

Sponged flames make a very handy "upsell"—a special upgrade to the job that allows you to charge a little more. A job this size without sponging normally goes for around $350, but by adding this simple technique, you can charge up to $500.

Before attempting this design on a vehicle, try practicing it on some old fenders. This is much cheaper than cleaning your mishaps off a customer's car and possibly ruining the base paint in the process! In this industry, some of the simplest designs and techniques can make you the most money if performed and promoted correctly!

Rose Art

Howie Nisgor

SUPPLIES

BRUSHES: Mack striping brushes, Alan Johnson
Signature Brush; #000, #0000 Xcaliber brushes,
Dick Blick Eclipse
PAINT MEDIA: 1-Shot® Lettering Enamel
OTHER: 1-Shot® Reducer (#6000),
Sunnyside turpentine and mineral spirits

Many times during the 46 years I've been pinstriping, people have found images in my designs that were not intended to be there. Sometimes, however, I like to incorporate specific images into my striping. This started back in 1969, when the owner of a drag race-car requested a pinstriped owl on the hood of his car. Drawing inspiration from pictorial striping by Dean Jeffries, and of course, the classic Von Dutch Rabbit, my ideas began to take shape. The recent pictorial work of Tramp Warner, Joe Sulty, and Alan Johnson also played a part in inspiring me to create this piece, a "Rose Art" pinstriping panel. I have already painted several versions of this basic design, and although they're similar in appearance, each panel is unique. The design of my "Rose Art" panel lends itself to a variety of additional possibilities, which I intend to pursue in the very near future.

1

2

3

4

5

6

Step 1

For this panel, I have selected factory-finished black 0.025 aluminum. I have pre-cut the panel to 13-inches by 24-inches to allow for a 2-inch border and 1-inch of uninterrupted black between the border and art areas. For safe handling, I clip all four corners at a 45-degree angle.

Step 2

I draw a 2-inch wide border on all four sides of the 13- by 24-inch black panel. Using a snap-off blade razor knife and metal edge layout triangle, I cut through the factory protective covering. Using the protective covering as a mask eliminates the additional masking step.

Step 3

I then carefully remove the mask from around the perimeter of the entire panel. For ease of removal, pull the mask back on itself, maintaining as low an angle as possible between mask and panel. You don't have to remove this as a single piece.

Step 4

After completely removing the mask, I thoroughly clean the entire exposed area with PPG Acryli-Clean DX 330 using paper towels. Be sure to remove the residue with a fresh paper towel—do not allow the cleaner to air dry.

Step 5

Using a 2-inch foam brush, I paint the border with a mixture of 1-Shot Reflex Blue Pearl paint with several drops of 1-Shot Bright Red added to warm the color slightly. I thinned the mixture using 1-Shot Reducer with a ratio of one part reducer to three parts paint.

Step 6

I immediately place a sheet of thin plastic on the wet paint surface. I use a cut-open supermarket produce bag to cover the entire panel, but you can also use clear plastic food wrap or dry cleaning bags turned inside-out to prevent the print from coming in contact with the paint.

7

8

9

10

11

12

Step 7

Quickly remove the bag from the wet paint surface. The paint will adhere to the bag and partially lift up from the panel surface, leaving behind a pattern similar in appearance to richly grained marble. The use of pearl paint gives the surface even more luster, adding to the illusion of dimension.

Step 8

To achieve a subtler marble pattern, turn the bag in on itself so that you can grip a clean section. Then bounce the crumpled bag repeatedly over the entire surface. This step softens and mottles the design of the border, resulting in a finer grain marble.

Step 9

Allow the pearl-marbled border to dry thoroughly and then remove the remaining mask from the panel. Once again, pull the mask back over itself, maintaining as low an angle as possible. A second pair of hands can prove very helpful at this point by securing the panel for greater ease in removal.

Step 10

Hold a paper pattern in place by using masking tape on all four corners. A trick is to cut football shaped pieces from the corners and place tape over

the top. This will make it much easier to place and remove the pattern. I slide yellow Saral transfer paper under the pattern. I then trace the pattern using a colored pen over the pencil line, making it easier to see which part of the pattern has already been drawn.

Step 11

Once the pattern is removed, you can easily see the basic rose design as a clear yellow line. Saral paper transfers a wax-free image onto almost any surface. You can use a conventional pounce pattern, but this leaves a powder residue on the surface. When I use a pounce pattern, I trace over it with a Stabilo pencil and gently wipe away all chalk before painting.

Step 12

I paint the basic "Rose Art" design using 1-Shot lettering enamels. I begin with the stem and leaf sections first. The colors are Process Green, Emerald Green, and custom mixed "Slime Green," which I make from one part Process Green and three parts Primrose Yellow.

13 14

Step 13

I start the rose itself using Rubine Red. Up to this point, I am following the lines of the basic pattern fairly closely. I also do not hesitate to turn the panel sideways or invert it to make painting easier. I do all the line work with sword stripers. I prefer Mack and #000 Xcaliber brushes, mixing paint and thinner on my palette.

Step 14

From this point on, I add additional colors using freehand pinstriping techniques. I also add some 1-Shot Magenta and Bright Red to the original Rubine Red. I outline the stem and leaf sections with Dark Green. This freehand line echoes the basic pattern, but also takes off on its own.

The finished "Rose Art" panel has freehand striping in a four-part blend, from Light Blue at the top to Reflex Blue at the bottom. I used highlight dots in tints to enhance the design. Note the gradual change from the Emerald Green stem to the Reflex Blue pinstripe. I also edge-striped the pearl-marbled border in Reflex Blue. My signature is in Bright Red with a matching red frame to compliment and complete this project.

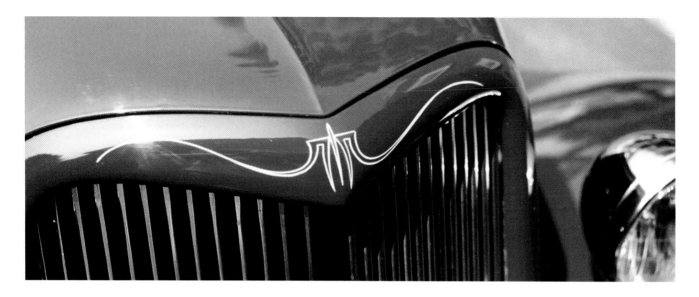

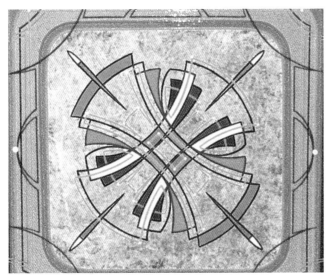

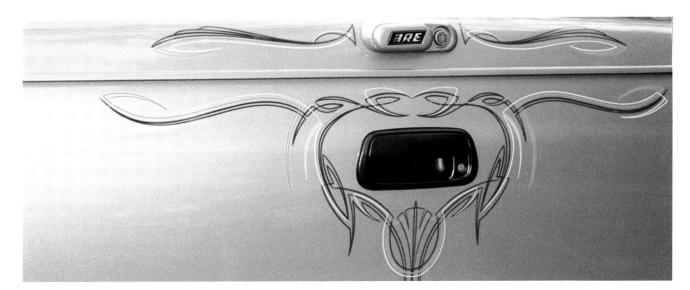

ROCK ON!

Paul Quinn

SUPPLIES

PAINT MEDIA: 1-Shot® Lettering Enamel,
DuPont powdered pearls

BRUSHES: #0 DC Flatliner, #2 Mack scrolling script,
#4 Quinn-Mack extended lettering quill

OTHER: Ardex 6214 Superfast Solvent;
3M™ Fine Line masking tape (#215); Stabilo pencil;
1-Shot® Hardener (#4007), Reducer (#6000),
Super Gloss Tinting Clear (#4006)

Recently, one of my regular customers, a body shop owner and top-notch guitarist, asked me to do a special job for him. He wanted to pay tribute to his late sister by naming and then decorating one of his guitars in her honor. Follow along as I combine lettering and striping techniques to make this guitar a truly unique showpiece.

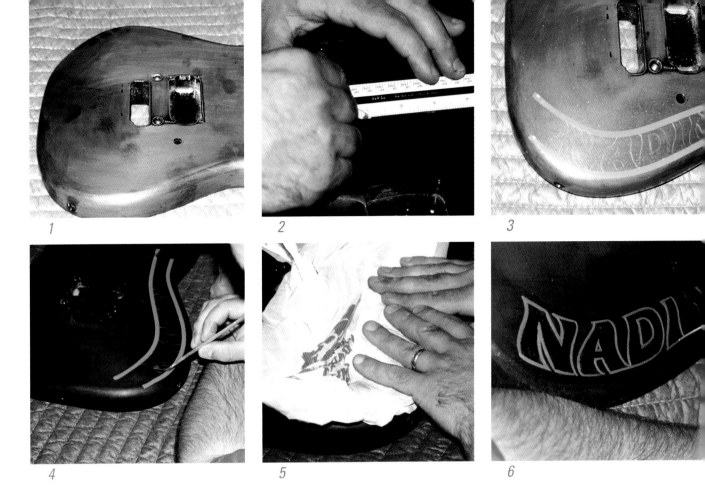

1   2   3

4   5   6

Step 1

The guitar body arrived at my shop, Design Brilliance, freshly painted, clearcoated, and wet-sanded flat—all ready for me to rock and roll!

Step 2

After wiping down the guitar with a wax and grease remover, I begin laying out some simple guidelines with a white Stabilo pencil for spacing purposes. The Stabilo is water-soluble, so you can easily remove these lines before applying the final clearcoat.

Step 3

Next, I lay the baseline and capline for the lettering of the name, Nadine. Following the curves of the guitar, I then draw the lettering using the Stabilo pencil.

Step 4

Using a Quinn-Mack extended lettering quill, I letter "Nadine" using 1-Shot Super Gloss Tinting Clear with a small amount of DuPont powdered pearl mixed in. I use 1-Shot reducers here, and because I will clearcoat the art with a urethane, I add 1-Shot Hardener, at about 10% by volume. Note the sparkle the pearl adds to the black base.

Step 5

Immediately upon completing the lettering, I "bag" the pearl using a plastic supermarket bag. You could also use plastic wrap for this technique. The finished look is a marblized "Nadine."

Step 6

After removing the blue tape, I mix some 1-Shot Metallic Gold with Purple to achieve a metallic burnt orange. I add hardener and reducer and outline "Nadine" using a #2 scrolling script brush by Mack.

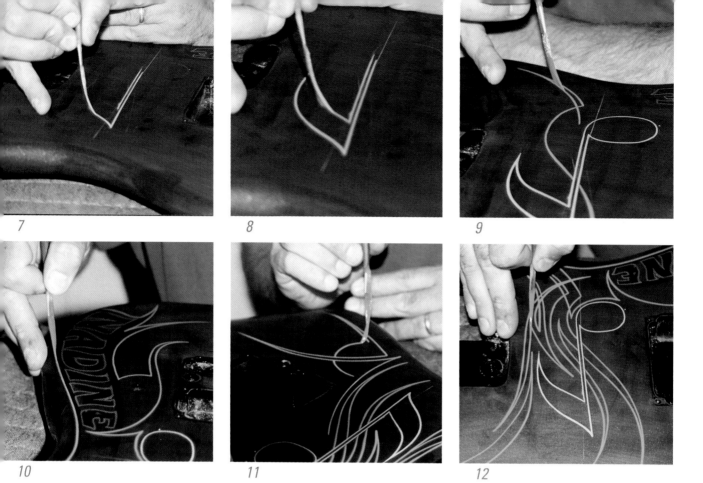

7

8

9

10

11

12

Step 7

Now that the lettering is done, I begin striping a music note, which will be the central point of the striping.

Step 8

For the striping, I use a #0 DC Flatliner striping brush by Mack. The color is a mix of 1-Shot Violet and Proper Purple. Note how my hands support the brush.

Step 9

The next color is Process Blue, with a drop or two of Proper Purple to warm it up a little.

Step 10

Because the guitar's shape differs from side to side, I go with an asymmetrical design. This allows me to work randomly with the body of the guitar. My goal is to achieve balance both in color and weight.

Step 11

I build upon the design using 1-Shot Process Green. Note how the brush is at a 90-degree angle to the surface and is on its tip for proper execution of the tight curve.

Step 12

I continue with the Process Green using a more traditional thumb and forefinger hold for more lengthy subtle curves.

Step 13

Changing to a mix of Proper Purple with some Violet (a darker mix than the music note), I continue to build upon the design. Because of the size and shape of the guitar, I can easily move around and stripe from all sides. This a welcome change after working in tight spots on cars and motorcycles!

Step 14

Adding a little more Violet to the mix, I build the design up with some teardrop-shaped accent lines.

All done! I leave the guitar to dry overnight, clearcoat it, wet-sand it, and polish it to a glass-like finish.

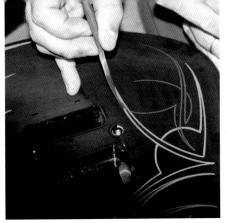

13

14

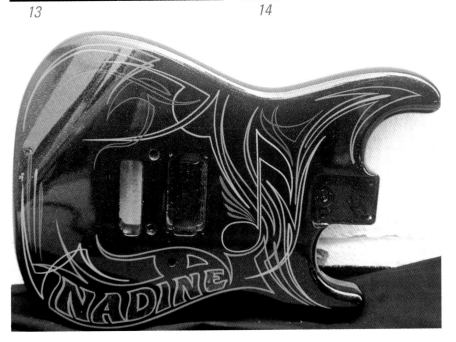

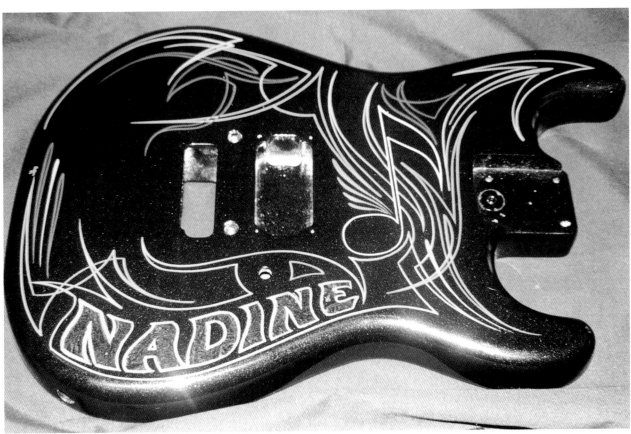

Living Large in Vegas
Bob Spena

SUPPLIES

PAINT MEDIA: 1-Shot® Lettering Enamel

BRUSHES: #3 French Master lettering quill,
#000 Mack striping brush

OTHER: Carbon pounce block, 3M™ Fine Line
masking tape (#215), 1-Shot sizing glue,
red variegated gold leaf, 24-carat gold leaf

Slinging paint since 1955, Bob Spena has been a fixture of hot rod pinstriping longer than many in the industry have been alive. It all started when Bob was 16 and his hero, Ed "Big Daddy" Roth, put him to work doing striping and sign painting. Bob also apprenticed under Kenneth "Von Dutch" Howard, who taught him the kustom painting end of the trade. Bob took a hiatus from painting after he was drafted into the Army during the Vietnam War, but when he returned, he had a job with Roth waiting for him. For the next ten years, Bob worked with Roth on the traveling show circuit. Around this time, Bob and Ed filmed a pinstripe how-to video starring Von Dutch.

This video, as well as numerous painting videos he made with Ed in the 1970s and '80s, established Bob as one of the first painters to encourage the educational aspect of the industry.

While many painters hopped from industry to industry over the years, Bob stayed true to his art form, practicing the same "old school" striping techniques he learned from the masters. You can still find him at his shop in Las Vegas, cranking out the lines. In this how-to, Bob paints one of his classic "Roth" panels in the old school style.

1   2   3

4   5   6

Step 1

Starting out with a pounce pattern of the famous Roth logo, Bob centers the design and tapes it down.

Step 2

Using a carbon pounce block, Bob transfers the design onto the sign blank.

Step 3

When using a carbon pounce, you must be careful not to smear the pounce line as you remove the pattern.

Step 4

With some blue fine line tape, Bob lays out some guidelines for the logo. These guidelines will mask off the straight lines of the lettering and keep the forms clean.

Step 5

To prepare for the gold leafing, Bob mixes up some 1-Shot sizing glue. The sizing glue adheres the gold leaf to the surface. He adds some gold pearl to the sizing to make it visible as it's being brushed on.

Step 6

Using a French Master #3 lettering quill, Bob brushes in the sizing glue along the masked guideline. Remember: Be careful with the sizing glue. Wherever the glue is, the gold leaf will stick!

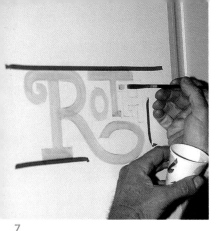

7

8

9

10

11

12

Step 7

The nice thing about a lettering quill is that you can get good 90-degree edge freehand with the squared-off brush.

Step 8

With the lettering done, Bob freehands in some curly-Q's and other old school goodies. The sizing is ready for the leaf when it's still sticky to the touch, but doesn't leave any residue on your finger. It will also make a squeaking noise when you drag your finger across it.

Step 9

For the curly-Q's and hot rod stripes, Bob uses some red variegated gold leaf, which is a composite leaf made from anodized aluminum with red streaks.

Step 10

Using the tissue backing in the leaf book, Bob places the leaf on the sizing. This protective tissue is needed for applying and burnishing in the leaf. The leaf is so thin that if you handle it with your bare fingers, you'll tear or damage it.

Step 11

Bob uses 24-carat gold leaf on the Roth logo. The leaf comes in a book of 25 sheets and is half the size of the composite. At $50 a book, the real leaf is also about four times the cost of the composite leaf.

Step 12

You can use either a soft brush or your fingers to remove the excess leaf and a damp cloth to wipe the surface down. This will help prevent loose pieces of leaf from flying all over and getting on other projects in your shop.

13

14

15

16

17

18

Step 13

With a piece of velvet wrapped around a cotton ball, Bob gives the gold a machine-turned look by spinning the velvet while pressing down against the leaf. This effect works best with real gold leaf, before the sizing completely sets.

Step 14

Using some 1-Shot Bright Red, Bob takes his #000 Mack brush and lays in a border around the panel. He draws the lines first and adds the radius corner later.

Step 15

In preparation for outlining the Roth logo, Bob lays in more tape guidelines to keep the edges clean.

Step 16

With some reduced 1-Shot Lettering Black, Bob gives the Roth logo a nice outline. This outline not only makes the lettering pop out, but it also cleans up the rough edge of the torn leaf.

Step 17

Keeping the brush wet with the black, Bob adds some extra striping around the hot rod leafing. By using only gold, black, and red, Bob keeps the design simple, a key component to old school striping.

Step 18

Switching back to the Mack sword striper, Bob lays in some traditional feathered pinstripe graphics with the red.

19

Step 19

Finishing off with the black, Bob continues elaborating on his original hot rod striping. The great thing about freehand striping is that you can continue to build on the design until you're happy with the final results.

While an old dog can learn new tricks, sometimes the best tricks are still handled by the old dogs!

Bob Spena with Ed "Big Daddy" Roth

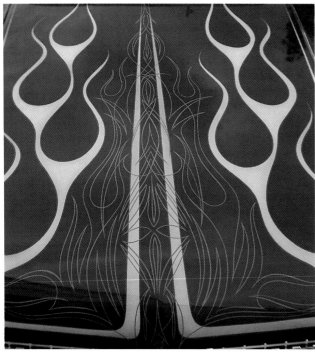

Von Franco

SUPPLIES

PAINT MEDIA: 1-Shot® Lettering Enamel
BRUSHES: Mack striping brushes
OTHER: Stabilo pencil, plastic cups, motor oil,
1-Shot® Low Temp Reducer (#6001)

Back in 1963, 13-year-old Frank Costanza rode his bike to the local auto show to see Rat Fink painting legend Ed "Big Daddy" Roth. After he showed Roth one of his own T-shirt designs (mostly done with a felt tip marker and rattle cans), Roth took the shirt and gave the boy a piece of paper with one word scribbled on it. Roth kept the shirt, saying it was the price for the secret, and that single word was all Frank needed to know.

The word was "Paasche," and three decades and countless Paasche airbrushes later, Frank, now known in the industry as Von Franco, still lives the kustom kulture lifestyle with a vengeance. Though most of Von Franco's work is now on canvas instead of T-shirts, his Roth-influenced style is still apparent. Merging the abstract art styles of Robert Williams, Ed Newton, and Basil Wolverton with the automotive pinstriping designs of Von Dutch, Ed Roth, and Larry Watson, Franco has created a synthesized art form that is as unique as any of his mentors' work.

Formerly a member of the Lucky Devils car club of Southern California, Von Franco recently joined the infamous Beatniks car club. Aside from their love of the color purple, the Beatniks are also known for the large number of kustom kulture artists who are members in good standing—Dennis McPhail, Jack Rudy, Daddy-O, and Rob Fortier, to mention just a few. After recently hosting a hot rod art show at the famous CBGB's nightclub in New York City, the Beatniks' reputation precedes them as the current key holders to Koolsville.

At first glance, Von Franco's work appears to be a fusion of '50s advertising art blended with the classic imagery of 1940s and '50s "B" movie posters. This retro style is not only timeless among the kustom kar crowd, but it is also making a name for itself in art galleries and among private collectors.

Get your brushes and join Von Franco for the creation of a quintessential kustom kulture design, a pinstriped Tiki.

1

2

3

4

5

6

Step 1

Before striping, Franco likes to sketch out the concept of his design.

Step 2

After many hours deciding on the proper canvas, Franco peels off a piece of the factory wood firewall in his Studebaker. Using a Stabilo, Franco sketches out the masterpiece for striping on his surface.

Step 3

Use a clean set of cups to mix your custom blend of reducers. Any contaminants may cause extremely dangerous reactions.

Step 4

For flow, Franco uses a little motor oil.

Step 5

One of the hardest things to do when striping is to actually get started, so Franco likes to add a little starter fluid.

Step 6

Franco likes this stuff because of the retro-logo on the can. He hasn't quite figured out what's in it yet, but it goes in anyway.

Step 7

Franco uses some 1-Shot Low Temp Reducer, which helps the striping flow better and stay wet longer for better line consistency.

Step 8

With 1-Shot, if you lose the lid, you don't have to worry—the paint makes one for you. Just take out your pocketknife and peel off the top skin.

Step 9

This is Franco's right-hand turn brush. He has properly trimmed the edges to make the brush stripe just right.

Step 10

Notice the proper squeegee technique when paletting the brush. This allows complete absorption of lead into the cuticle.

Step 11

A good hand position is important. Using one hand as a guide and the other hand to steady himself, Franco is able to follow his sketch with nice clean even strokes. If you properly palette your brush, you can make the majority of these lines without having to re-palette.

Step 12

Unlike a pen and ink design, the pinstripe design has a nice contoured shape. Starting and ending with a point, these lines are what give the design its character. Of course, knowing how to pull them is also beneficial.

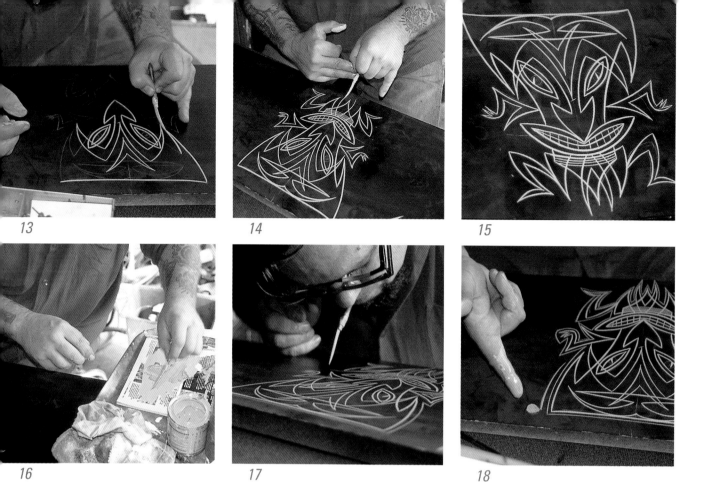

13

14

15

16

17

18

Step 13

Franco is the master of creating these pinstripe characters. Although he sketched this one in advance, he creates many designs as he stripes. When something in the design catches his eye, he works with it to "bring it out."

Step 14

Near the end of the design, Franco adds teeth and a few extra lines that were not in the original sketch. A good sketch is a great way to start the design process, but it should not end there—you should always modify your design, adding or subtracting from it throughout the creation process.

Step 15

Here's the completed design in all its Tiki glory! Because this design was done with 1-Shot, you need to remember that the paint will remain wet for at least a few hours.

Step 16

Adding some turquoise 1-Shot to the yellow palette, Franco makes a nice dirty lime green to finish off the design.

Step 17

Franco demonstrates his favorite Von Dutch striping technique. Using the classic mouth brush style, he shows us how to impress the competition, make friends, and actually stripe without reading glasses.

Step 18

Sneezing is a common problem while using the mouth brush technique. Many would view this blob of paint as a major setback, and some may even try to fix it. You must view all your mistakes as art. Heck, even charge more for them if you can!

There you have it! Nice signature, cool Tiki, and even the brush becomes part of the design, after it is accidentally left there for a few hours. Jackson Pollack could not have been more proud. The only sad note is that Franco really liked that brush.

Von Franco

Von Franco

Motorcycle Graphics and Striping
Wizard

SUPPLIES

PAINT MEDIA: 1-Shot® Lettering Enamel
BRUSHES: Mack and Mike Lavallee striping brushes

After working in the motorcycle market for 30 years, I've learned some things that can make or break a striper in this business. I will share some of my knowledge with you as I take you along for the creation of this small fender art design. First of all, bikers are just like hot rodders, except they have more tattoos and bigger, more threatening biceps! Bikers like tough-looking graphics, and their imposing presence often brings out the best in a striper. The graphic that I'm walking you through here is a Southwestern art piece that I have done several hundred times over the years, in varying degrees of detail. It nicely graces the front fender of a bike, but also does well on the trunk of a "bagger" or downsized on the rear fender. Let's begin!

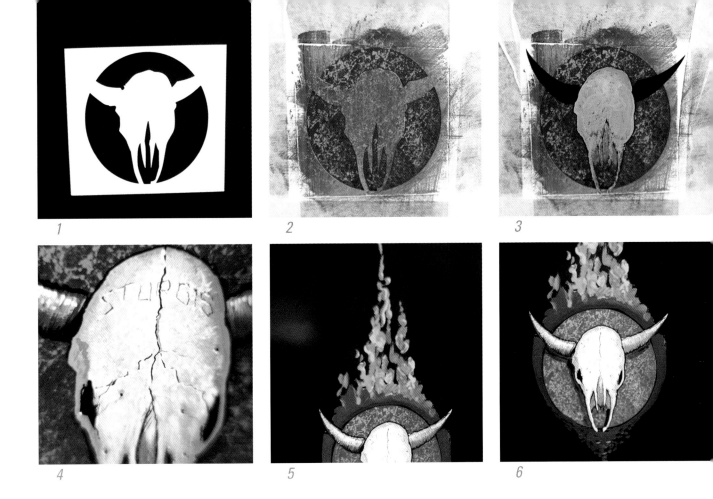

1

2

3

4

5

6

Step 1

First, after sketching the outline of the steer skull on paper, I scan the sketch into my computer and clean it up. I also add an oval outline to the design so I can cut several of them to accommodate later jobs. I then apply the stencil to the center of the fender. This is no time to be lazy—make sure you center it well.

Step 2

After masking off the outer edges, I apply several shades of blue to indicate a sky background. I then sponge in a lighter shade of 1-Shot Aqua, just to make the background more interesting. Note: Don't get too ambitious here. The foreground should be much more interesting than the background.

Step 3

Next, I peel off the skull shape and begin applying a light base of 1-Shot tan to fill in some color. (You have to work very fast, as the enamel base dries quickly and blending is a must.) I palette in some ivory, using very light, tapping strokes to give the appearance of a bone that is rough and dried out. I'm not looking for a smooth blend here—I'm throwing in highlights by adding more ivory to the center of the skull. Notice the shadows around the left side of the skull already. Working dark to light gives you built-in shadows.

Step 4

This close-up shows details of cracks and lettering that look carved into the skull.

Step 5

I "chase" a layer of maroon with Orange, Fire Red, and Vermillion to indicate a flame outline. Proper Purple cools off the design at the bottom.

Step 6

This step gives the skull depth. A mixture of clearcoat and a drop of Lettering Black make a glaze for a shadow, which makes the skull "float" off the surface.

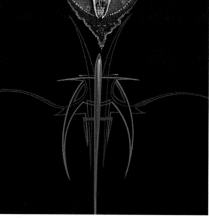

7

8

Step 7

I add beads with drops of 1-Shot Blue Green and highlight them with aqua and do the same for the red and orange beads. Also, a thin Process Blue outline makes this graphic clean and appealing.

Step 8

Next, I add striping for garnish. This step requires thought—do you stripe the tanks and fenders to finish the bike? Don't get carried away with striping until the graphic disappears. If it's done well, the striping sells itself.

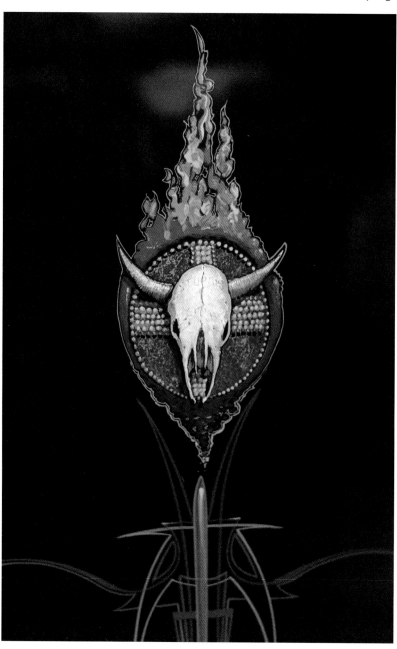

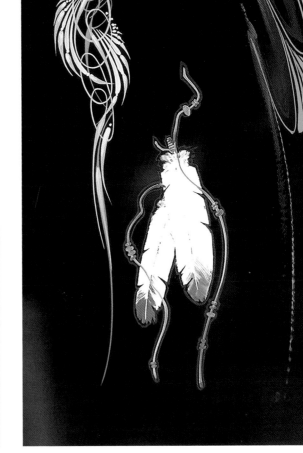

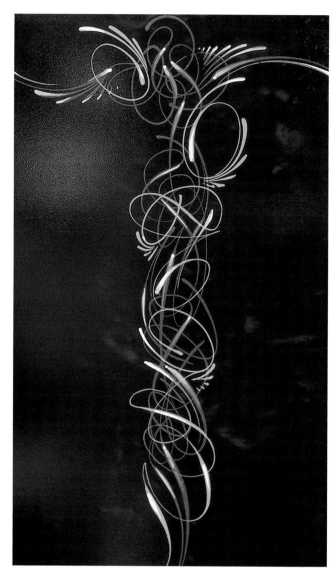

Index

159

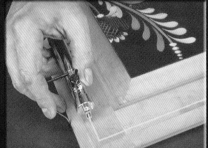

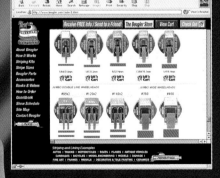
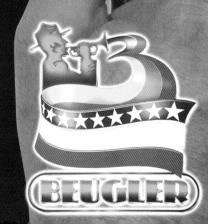

CREATEX AUTO AIR COLORS
THE WATERBORNE REVOLUTION!

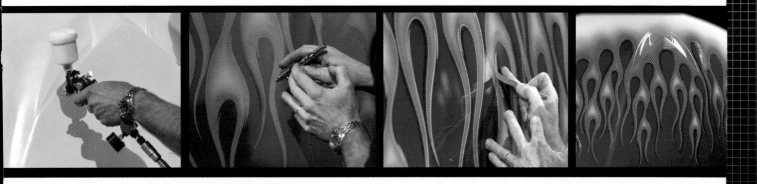

AUTOMOTIVE BASE COAT GRAPHIC BASE PAINT

Auto Air Colors are ready to spray base coat graphic paints available in over 115 colors. Brilliant and durable, Auto Air Colors are an intermixable system for creating limitless custom effects with greater flexibility than urethane and lacquer paints making them more resistant to chipping and flaking. Auto Air Colors have been reformulated and improved. Colors now spray smoother than ever before and dry to a smooth, flat finish. Colors do not require additives and are fully compatible with virtually any urethane or polyurethane automotive clear. Also available is the new Auto Air Colors User Guide Video and DVD.

. WATERBORNE

. LIGHTFAST

. PERMANENT

. NON-TOXIC

. ECONOMICAL

. CANDY COLORS

CREATEX™

www.autoaircolors.com
1.800.509.6563

sit our website or call to order a color chart, technical guide & instructional video.